# I Will Live.
# My Children
# Need Me.

## Charles Brady

# DEDICATION

I dedicate this book to the wonderful doctors and nurses of Point Pleasant Hospital who saved Carmie from certain death upon the birth of my first son. Without their love and expertise, I would not have a family about which to write. There would be no "Brady Bunch".

I dedicate this book to the wonderful doctors and nurses and to the entire staff of Columbia Presbyterian Hospital. After doctors from all over the metropolitan area had sentenced Carmie to two months to live, the doctors at Columbia Presbyterian not only gave her hope, but cured her of what had been diagnosed as "incurable cancer". Without the love and expertise of those wonderful doctors, this book could not have been written.

I dedicate this book to Maria, Carmie's spiritual healer who brought Carmie closer to God than she had ever been in her life. Without Maria, Carmie would not have had the strength and faith to overcome certain death.

I dedicate this book to Carmie's mother and father, Bob and Dot, to "The Juniors" and to all of Carmie's wonderful friends whose love and encouragement constantly reinforced Carmie's will to live for her children. Without their love, Carmie's laughter would have ended at age thirty five.

Finally, I dedicate this book to my wonderful sons: Matthew, Scott, and Patrick. In Mom's last words, "We did a good job."

# INTRODUCTION

*"I will live. My children need me."*
*—Carmie Brady*

# Who Is Carmie Brady?

On the boardwalk in Point Pleasant, New Jersey, sits a bench that is dedicated to the life and love of Carmie Brady. Inscribed on the bench are the words, "Laughing, Loving, Caring," words that sum up the life of this remarkable woman. Whenever people talk about Carmie, the first qualities they mention are her loud and somewhat infectious laugh, her caring personality, and the love that she shared with everyone she met.

Carmie was the recipient of many miracles throughout her life. After her passage into eternal life, she became an instrument through whom God has granted the gift of miracles to those who have prayed to her. It has taken me five years to write this book. Most of the days were spent typing through tears or typing with a huge smile on my face. I now realize that I have created a love story that is summed up in the title, "I will live. My children need me."

At age twenty-eight, Carmie faced almost certain death during the birth of her first son. The attending physician later stated, "The fact that Carmelinda and Matthew lived is truly a miracle."

At age thirty-five, Carmie was diagnosed as having a rare form of breast cancer and was given two months to live. Doctor after doctor gave her the same verdict: "The cancer is not operable. You have two months to live." Through her faith in God, her determination to live for her three little sons, and what the surgeon referred to as a "miracle," Carmie lived and was cancer-free for fifteen years.

At age forty-five, Carmie realized that God had kept her alive for a reason. She returned to college and received her master's degree in mental health counseling. She devoted the rest of her life to helping  unfortunate clients who were desperately in need of her love.

At age forty-eight, Carmie was diagnosed as having ovarian cancer. The doctors were amazed at the number of times she went into remission and continued to counsel her patients. Her work on earth was not yet completed.

If you or a loved one are staring death in the face or suffering from serious illness, if you feel like you cannot cope with the situation in which you find yourself, if you have lost faith in God and your fellow human beings, if you feel like the world is sitting on your shoulders, this book is a must-read. My prayer for you is that, somewhere within the pages of this book, you will find the courage, strength, and faith to overcome your fears and doubts.

*Charles A Brady*  [Husband-Author]

# Table of Contents

# Chapter 1

# How We Met

## *1973*

In order to adequately portray our chance meeting and the beautiful life that we experienced together, I must first step back into the past. As a child, I attended Our Lady of Lourdes grammar school in West Orange and St. Benedict's Preparatory School in Newark. I graduated from Seton Hall University in South Orange in 1958 and took a position in the marketing department of a large gas company.

Driven by an insatiable desire to serve God and to help others, I entered a seminary and was ordained to the Catholic priesthood in 1966. As a priest in the 1960s, I served in two predominantly black parishes in Orange and Montclair, New Jersey, where I taught Dr. Martin Luther King Jr.'s philosophy of love and brotherhood to the children of the area.

I reached the youth by building pride through athletics. I am proud of the fact that our youth programs, which were coordinated by Father Jack Sullivan and me, won three national championships, four Eastern States championships, eight state championships, and twenty-eight county championships in seven years. Many of the young people who participated in the programs went on to excel in college in both academics and sports.

My commitment to the civil rights movement caused Coretta Scott King to write a note to me on the inside flap of her book, *My Life with Martin Luther King*: "Charley, with deep appreciation for your love and support of those ideals of love, justice, truth, peace, and brotherhood. May our common efforts hasten the day when Martin's dream will be realized. Coretta Scott."

After seven years and much prayer and soul-searching, I resigned from active priesthood—but not the church—for reasons that I will now divulge. I had thousands of children participating in my programs, and they all called me Father. Yet something was missing. The truth is that I yearned to have a loving wife and children of my own.

I want to make it clear that I did not leave the church, nor did I abandon my faith in God. My years in the priesthood were a major part of my life that I will always cherish. Just as I felt that I had a divine calling to enter the priesthood, I now feel that I have a divine calling to serve God in another way.

Carmie grew up in the Vailsburg section of Newark. She attended Sacred Heart grammar school and East Orange Catholic High School, where she was a wiz in mathematics. Upon graduation, she was offered a position in the underwriting division of Prudential Insurance Company. The company offered to train her to be an underwriter and to pay her way through college. She decided that she would not be happy in that tedious profession and enrolled in Seton Hall University where she majored in social studies.

After graduation from college, Carmie took a job at Prudential Property and Casualty Insurance Company as a systems analyst trainee for less money than she would have received out of high school; but she was happy. Her fellow employees were in awe of the fact that, although she hardly knew how to use a computer, she singlehandedly wrote the specs for all of the property and casualty software in the company. One of her friends marveled,

"Carmie has a mind like a computer." Carmie very quickly worked her way into management, where she remained until she resigned in order to care for her children.

A few months after I resigned from active ministry, I was sipping a drink in the Ship Wheel, which was one of the "in" places at the Jersey Shore. I feel quite certain that I was led to the Ship Wheel by the Holy Spirit. Suddenly, I became aware of infectious, indescribably beautiful laughter coming from across the room. I looked around and saw a gorgeous young lady standing with her girlfriends, laughing her heart out. I immediately noticed that those standing nearby were joining in her laughter.

After returning my attention to my drink, I soon became aware that the contagious laughter was now close behind me. The Holy Spirit told me to get up and offer my seat to the woman with the laugh. Of course, I immediately obeyed. It was then that I noticed that she had beautiful, long hair and gorgeous eyes. As I attempted to make conversation, it became apparent to me that she was very shy. I don't know why; but, I introduced myself to her as Chuck instead of Charley. From that day on I became Chuck to everyone I met.

As we conversed, she quietly said to me, "I don't usually talk to men." After chatting with her for a while, I found out that she was only twenty-two years of age. Since I was embarrassed about being thirty-nine and really liked this young woman, I lied to her. I told her that I was thirty-eight. (I have always been told that I look at least twelve years younger than my actual age.) What I did know was that she liked me and was very comfortable with me. As for me, it was love at first sight. She was as beautiful inside as she was outside.

The following night, I took Carmie out to dinner at the dollar buffet at the Ship Wheel. Needless to say, there was very little laughter. Carmie would later tell me, "I couldn't believe I was out with an old cheapskate." For the rest of her life, she never let me forget about the dollar buffet.

The next night, I took her to a beautiful restaurant and confessed that I had lied about my age. "I'm really thirty-nine," I said.

She laughed hysterically. "You lied to me for one year? What's the difference between thirty-eight and thirty-nine?"

The very next day, Carmie took me to meet her mother and stepfather, Bob and Dorothy Rostoff. Bob and Dot, as we affectionately called them, had been recently married and lived in a beautiful home on the water in Point Pleasant. Despite my age and the fact that I was an ex-priest, I was immediately accepted into the family. I loved them from the moment I met them.

Carmie and I dated for over a year and were very much in love with each other.

# CHAPTER 2

# United in God's Love

## *July 12, 1975*

Carmie's birthday was March twelfth. Mine was June twelfth. We were married at lawn party at Carmie's cousin's home in Sea Girt, New Jersey, on July twelfth—in the midst of a tropical storm.

Carmie called me early in the morning, weeping. "Chuck, our day is ruined. It's pouring out. There are thunder and lightning and forty-mile-an-hour winds." She was crying her eyes out.

I said a quick prayer and then made her a promise. "I promise you that the sun will shine when you walk down the aisle. In fact, I'll bet you a hundred dollars that the sun will be shining."

A red, antique Rolls Royce delivered Carmie to the house in Sea Girt. As she arrived, the clouds parted, and the sun burst through the clouds in all its brilliant splendor. When you hear about how God took care of this beautiful woman throughout her life, I'm sure you'll agree that the parting of the clouds at her wedding was an act of divine intervention.

As Carmie walked down the aisle, dressed in her beautiful white gown and carrying a petite parasol, I heard people gasp at her beauty and her gorgeous smile.

Father Lutz, with whom I served as a priest, was waiting under the tent at the end of the aisle, dressed in African garb known as a dashiki. With him was his young, black son. The boy's parents had abandoned him at a young age, so this saintly priest had taken the child in and adopted him.

Carmie and I exchanged vows and walked down the aisle into the bright sunlight that the Holy Spirit had provided for us on our special day.

**Carmie pays off $100 bet about the weather.**

Our wedding photos were taken in the beautiful, sunlit gardens until the heavens once again roared with thunder. The skies lit up with piercing lightning. The wind howled fiercely at over fifty miles per hour. Joyfully, we crammed into the tent for what was to become one of the most festive weddings that anyone could ever imagine.

8

# Chapter 3

# The First Miracle

## *1980*

Carmie and I had been happily married for over four years when we decided that, because of my age, we should have a baby before it was too late. I think I hit a home run on the first try. After all those years of celibacy, nothing was going to stop it.

I will never forget the day Carmie returned from her regular checkup with her doctor. She burst through the door. "Chuck, I'm so excited. I'm pregnant! We're going to have a baby." We hugged and kissed and went to celebrate at the very place where we had met—the Ship Wheel.

Carmie had been seeing her doctor regularly. He assured her that she was in good health. Since this was our first pregnancy, we took his word for it. In hindsight, I remember the admonition of the Lamaze instructor who was a nurse at the same hospital as the doctor. "Whatever you do, don't go to Point Pleasant Hospital. The doctors are inferior." Almost in the same breath, she cautioned, "I'm worried about you, Carmie. Your face and arms are dangerously swollen, and you are obviously filling up with fluid."

Resting her arm on a table or her leg on a chair would result in a huge indentation on her arm or leg. Something was not right. People were urging her to go see her doctor immediately. Carmie had been seeing the doctor every week, and yet he said nothing about the swelling. On July 1, 1980, she felt so sick that she insisted on seeing the

9

doctor. "Doctor, my arms and legs are swollen. I have diarrhea, and I'm sick to my stomach. I have a terrible pain in the back of my head. I feel horrible."

The doctor stated, "There is nothing wrong with you. This is simply the baby moving down, and it is very normal. If you want to have the baby, this is what you must put up with."

On July third, Carmie could no longer stand the pain in the back of her neck and the ravages of constant diarrhea. She called the doctor, who prescribed over-the-counter medicine for the diarrhea and the pain in the back of her neck. There was no relief. She sat up in bed all night, her body wracked with pain. I must have dozed off.

All of a sudden, I woke with a start. The entire bed was shaking. I thought the cat was jumping around on my feet.

"Damn it, get out of here," I yelled.

I became absolutely terrified when I heard a loud snoring sound coming from deep in Carmie's throat. When I jumped out of bed and flipped on the light, I saw the most horrible and terrifying sight that I have ever seen in my life. Carmie's face and head were grotesquely swollen. Her tongue was swollen out of her mouth, and her eyes were rolled back in her head. Foam and vomit were gurgling out of her mouth. Her entire body was quaking with convulsions.

"Carmie, Carmie, Carmie, wake up!"

I thought she was in cardiac arrest. I immediately thought of the baby and blew air into Carmie's mouth and lungs. I dialed the operator to call the police. Unfortunately, this was the only way to call the police department prior to the inception of 9-1-1. There was no answer. They must have been working with a skeleton crew on the Fourth of July morning. I screamed out the window. "Help, please, my wife and baby are dying. Call the police!"

No one answered. Over and over, I blew air into Carmie's lungs and dialed the operator. After what seemed like an eternity, the operator answered. I screamed, "Call the police and emergency squad. My wife is having a heart attack. She is pregnant!"

When the police dispatcher answered, I cried, "My wife is pregnant. She is having a heart attack. Bring oxygen!"

Within one minute, a young cop burst through the door with an oxygen tank, and he immediately administered oxygen to Carmie and the baby. When the emergency squad arrived, they were afraid to touch Carmie. They thought she had severe sunburn because her skin was scarlet red. They did not know if they could lift her, because she was so bloated. We were only three blocks from the local hospital.

Remembering the words of the Lamaze instructor, I begged the ambulance driver, "Please take her to another hospital. I don't want her to go to Point Pleasant."

The driver retorted, "Mister, this lady won't make it to another hospital."

We arrived at the emergency room at about 3:00 a.m. Carmie was convulsing wildly. By some miracle, Dr. Dwyer and Dr. Ketelaar were in the hospital. They had performed seventeen deliveries during the past day and night and were leaving for a well-earned rest. At the time, I didn't know who these doctors were.

I saw Dr. Dwyer rip open Carmie's gown and proceed to administer CPR. He gave orders to the nurses to call the cardiologist and neurologist. "This girl is in complete eclampsia!"

The doctor rushed over to me. I thought he was going to hit me. "When was the last time this girl saw a doctor?"

With my voice trembling, I said, "She had an internal exam just last week and saw her doctor again three days ago. She spoke on the phone with her doctor again yesterday because of the constant diarrhea and vomiting and a terrible pain in the back of her neck. He recommended that I go to the drugstore and purchase over-the-counter medicine."

Dr. Dwyer's face turned scarlet. "What?" he blurted and rushed back to Carmie's side.

When the convulsions temporarily subsided, Dr. Dwyer came out to me and explained. "Your wife's blood pressure has gone through the roof. Her brain is dangerously swollen. She is filled with fluid. We have already drained seven pints of fluid from her body. She has what we call 'complete eclampsia.' We don't know what causes it, but it's something you only see in the Deep South and in poverty-stricken areas where medical attention is not readily available. Eclampsia is the result of toxemia that has been neglected."

"If we do not stop the convulsions and lower the blood pressure immediately, she will die. The only way to stop the convulsions is to take the baby by caesarean section. There is a very strong chance that both your wife and baby will die. We have no choice but to operate immediately if we are to save your wife and child."

Dr. Dwyer then placed his hand on my shoulder and gently squeezed it. With utmost compassion he said gently, "This is normally a very rewarding and joyful profession. Helping to bring a child into the world is a thrill that I will always cherish. This is very difficult for me. I promise that I will do everything in my power to save your wife and baby."

At that moment, I knew that the ambulance driver's decision to bring us to Point Pleasant hospital was best for us.

There was nothing left to do but pray. I remember standing with Bob Rostoff, Carmie's stepfather, in a converted closet that served as the "father's room." I remember him saying, "You say some Christian prayers. I'll say some Jewish prayers." The two of us prayed and prayed as we waited.

After what seemed like an eternity, a joyful nurse burst through the door with my newborn son in her arms. "You have a beautiful healthy boy." She placed the child in my arms. Bob and I wept openly and thanked God for this wonderful miracle. Matthew Charles Brady was born on July fourth (7/4) at 7:40 a.m. Bible scholars will confirm that *seven* and *four* are considered to be perfect numbers in the Bible. This was truly a sign that a miracle was being bestowed upon us by our merciful God.

Dr. Dwyer came into the room and put his arm around me. "Don't look back and wonder," he said. "This is a perfectly healthy baby. There are no ill effects from the trauma that he has been exposed to."

The joy was not to last. Dr. Ketelaar gently took me aside. "I am very sorry, Mr. Brady," he said nervously. "Your wife is still in a coma and convulsing wildly. If she has another series of convulsions, in all likelihood her blood will coagulate, or she will suffer a severe stroke. Both would most likely end in death."

At about 10:00 a.m., Dr. Ketelaar came to me and said compassionately, "You've been up all night. There is nothing you can do. Go home and get some rest."

There was nothing I could do but pray. I never prayed so hard in my life. Carmie and Matthew were now in God's hands. I went home and sat on my front steps. I wept and prayed. "God, please don't let Carmie die. I can't live without her. Please, by some miracle, give me back my wife. Matthew needs his mother. I need my wife."

Something told me to look to my left. Next to me was a five-year-old rosebush that had never bloomed. At that time, I was on the test panel of Jackson Perkins Rose Company. The bush would grow huge buds, but they would never open and bloom. A horticulturist from Jackson Perkins advised me to cut the bush down. "It will never bloom. It is defective."

On that bush was a huge, red rose. That rose was truly a sign from God that a miracle was taking place. I knew immediately that Carmie and the baby were going to live. I got on my knees and prayed, "Thank you, Jesus."

**Actual picture of the rose that bloomed on 7/4 at 7:40 a.m.**

When I returned to the hospital, Dr. Ketelaar told me that Carmie had suffered through four more seizures. In a bewildered voice, he exclaimed, "All of a sudden, the seizures stopped. I don't know why. I can't explain it."

For three days, Carmie was kept in the delivery room because she was in such critical condition and still in a coma. The wonderful doctors ate and slept in the room. They and the nurses remained by her side throughout the

Fourth of July holiday. Mrs. Brown, the head nurse, even missed her own Fourth of July party. As if by an act of God, no more babies were born during those three days. It was as if God wanted Carmie to have the full attention of the doctors and nurses.

My mother later told me that she had prayed for three days before a shrine to the Blessed Virgin that I had built in her back yard: "Blessed Mother, you have to help that girl. Don't let her die. My son and baby need her." Then my mother lit a votive candle that was manufactured to burn for three hours. The candle burned for the entire three days that Carmie was lying in a coma.

# CHAPTER 4

# The First Bottle

Matthew was ready for his first bottle. A nurse came to me with Matthew in her arms. "Sit down here and hold Matthew. For a while, you are going to be his mother and his father. I will teach you everything you need to know."

For the whole time that Carmie was in the delivery room, I returned to the hospital for each feeding. For the short time that I was holding that blessed child, the anguish and fear that was in my heart turned to joy and jubilation. I was caressing and feeding God's gift to Carmie and me and to the whole world.

One day while I was feeding Matthew, a nurse came to me and took him in her arms. "We are moving Carmie to the intensive care unit. She is still in a coma. You can see her now."

Carmie was lying on a gurney outside of the delivery room. I cannot express the anguish and fear that was in my heart. I kissed her and said, "Hi, Carmie. You are going to be well. You had a baby boy." I felt a strange feeling of electricity flowing from my body to hers. It was the same feeling that I had often experienced as a priest when I was praying over sick people.

Carmie instantly woke up, smiled, and groggily said, "Hi"—as if nothing had happened. The nurse held the baby to her face and said, "Carmie, this is your baby. He is beautiful."

Carmie smiled as only a mother could smile. "Ooooh," she said and smiled some more. I did not realize at the time that she could not see Matthew or me. She was blind and paralyzed on one side.

On the evening of July twelfth, Carmie was still in ICU. I returned to the hospital for the evening feeding. Dr. Dwyer was waiting for me. He told me that I could not feed Matthew that night and that I should go to a certain room. As I sat in the empty room wondering what could be wrong, I remembered that it was our fifth wedding anniversary.

Suddenly Dr. Dwyer burst through the door with a big smile on his face. He was pushing Carmie in a wheelchair. She was still a very sick young lady. The swelling had subsided; but, her paralyzed arm drooped by her side. I was elated to see that her eyes were wide open and she could see again. She had the biggest and most beautiful smile I had ever seen. I hugged her and said, "I love you, Carmie. Happy anniversary." We hugged and cried and hugged some more.

Dr. Dwyer left the room and returned moments later with little Matthew in his arms. He gently placed Matthew on Carmie's lap. She smiled and sighed as she gazed upon her beautiful son for the first time. She tenderly reached out with the arm that had only moments before been paralyzed and hung limp at her side. She held God's gift in her arms. Through that loving doctor, another miracle had taken place. Smiling from ear to ear, she fed him the baby bottle. When he fell asleep, the nurses took him from Carmie and returned him to his crib. Next, they served us a steak dinner, complete with candlelight and champagne.

I remember begging the doctors and nurses not to send Matthew home prior to Carmie's release. I wouldn't have known how to care for him. The nurses held daily classes to teach me how—among other things—to change a messy diaper.

Finally, the day came when Carmie and Matthew were to be released from the hospital.. Dr. Dwyer sat us both down. "Carmelinda, you are still a very sick young lady. We will have to monitor your blood pressure for the rest of your life. You will remain on phenobarbital to prevent the swelling of the brain from recurring and to control your blood pressure. You are not to lift the baby for three months. Chuck, you will be mother and father to Matthew for as long as it takes." As we left the hospital, nurses and doctors from all over the hospital came to see the "miracle baby" and to wish us well.

There would be many months of rehabilitation and difficulties, but our prayers had been answered. Think of it. Two wonderful doctors, who had just assisted in seventeen births, were still in the hospital at 3:00 a.m. on the morning of the Fourth of July. There were no births during the three days that followed, while Carmie lay in a coma in the delivery room. Matthew was born On July fourth [7/4] at 7:40. A votive candle meant to burn for three hours burned for three days. A big, red rose bloomed at the time of Matthew's birth on a defective bush that was to be chopped down. With the arm that was paralyzed, this new mother reached out and lovingly held her beautiful baby.

To this day, the doctors and nurses marvel about the miracle they witnessed on 7/4/1980 at 7:40 a.m. In the words of Dr. Dwyer, "I will never forget Matt's birth on July 4, 1980. The fact that Matthew and Carmelinda lived is truly a miracle."

Carmie's loving mother and stepfather invited us to stay at their house during the rehabilitation. Carmie and her mother Dorothy had a bond that is the dream of every mother and daughter. Dorothy was beautiful, inside and out, and was, without a doubt, one of the most wonderful women I have ever met. Dot, as she was known, took care of Matthew while I was at work. She fed and changed him and performed all the tasks that were usually reserved for the mother. I had the night shift—the crying baby awake in the night, dirty diapers, and endless hours of sleepless nights.

Oftentimes, my wonderful father-in-law, Bob, would come into the room and send me back to bed while he fed Matthew and changed his dirty diaper. Bob was most certainly a unique person. He was only about five feet, eight inches tall, but he had a fifty-four-inch chest and a thirty-eight-inch waist. He had a bald head, huge eyebrows, eyes that could pierce armor, a huge handlebar mustache, and more hair on his body than any ape I have ever seen. He had a second-degree black belt in karate, was a scuba diving instructor, and could bench-press over three hundred and fifty pounds.

I can still picture the scene. There he was—this massive, hairy grandfather, sitting in his pajama bottoms, tenderly caressing his grandson and feeding him his bottle. As I dozed off to sleep, I could hear him singing lullabies in the same Yiddish language that his own mother must have sung to him when he was a child.

I often hear about how important it is for a mother and father to bond with their child from the very moment the child is born. Matt must have bonded with Bob and Dot from the very beginning of his life. Little did they know that the acts of love they bestowed on that little baby at the beginning of his life would be returned to them a hundredfold. I do not think that any grandchild has ever loved and done as much for his grandparents as Matt did.

When Bob had a stroke at age sixty-seven, Matt visited him every day in the hospital. When Bob was moved to the rehab center, Matt was there for him every day. Bob was determined to make himself better through constant and painstaking exercises. Matt was always there with him, helping him exercise his muscles and encouraging him when he would become despondent. "Come on, Poppy. You can do it. Come on; one more time. Push-lift-pull!" Matt nursed Bob as faithfully as his grandfather had nursed him as a child. Matt was with Bob right up until the end of his life, when Matt finally told him, "You can let go, Poppy. I promise you that I will take care of Nana."

When Dot grew old, Matt was always there for her. He took her to the mall, to the food store, to the doctors, and to the hairdresser. When he could have been out with his friends, he ate dinner with her and listened to her problems. As time passed, she suffered from dementia. For over two years, Matt was her caretaker. He arranged for a caretaker to live with her and cook for her. Nana would call at all times of the day or night, and Matt would run to her side.

One time I heard the garage door open in the middle of the night. Matt had been out to a party and had a few drinks. When I ran down the stairs, I saw Matt taking his bike out into the pouring rain. I yelled, "Matt, where are you going?"

It was two o'clock in the morning, and he answered, "Nana called. She needs me. I am going over there." When I tried to stop him, he blurted, "I have to go. It's my job." Matt rode the bike over five miles in the dark and pouring rain because he loved her so much.

The first thing we did when we moved back into our own home was to throw a huge party to celebrate our little miracle. Many of the doctors and nurses, who were God's instruments in our miracle, attended the party and took turns holding and kissing Matthew.

I will never forget the first time Carmie changed a diaper. It was the smelliest, dirtiest diaper that anyone could imagine. I gagged and choked. "I can't do this," I said. "I am going to throw up!" Carmie laughed and laughed. "I'll change the diaper." She laughed the whole time she was changing the diaper. From that day on, it was pure teamwork. I changed the easy ones.

Dr. Dwyer called us to his office and warned us, "You are not to have any more children. There is a danger that the swelling of the brain and the high blood pressure will recur." His orders were not to be. God had other plans for us. We were blessed with two more miracles. Scott was born on March 30, 1982 by C- Section, and Patrick was born on April 18, 1984. Both were high-risk births. Toward the end of both pregnancies, I was often afraid to go to sleep at night. The trauma of Matthew's birth appeared over and over again in my head.

Patrick's birth was also planned to be by C-section. Before the procedure could take place, I was awakened in the night by Carmie's boisterous laughter. "Chuck, my water just broke."

Needless to say, I went into a panic. "Call Dr. Dwyer! Call an ambulance!" Carmie was laughing hysterically at me. Her water had broken during a high-risk pregnancy, and she was actually laughing and making fun of me.

Carmie picked up the phone and calmly called Dr. Dwyer. "Doctor, I am sorry to call you during the night, but my water just broke." By now, there was a special bond developing between Carmie and Dr. Dwyer. "Great timing, Carmelinda," he said, laughingly. "I am leaving for vacation tomorrow. Get to the hospital immediately."

Until the day she died, Carmie laughed her heart out whenever she told her friends about the events that happened next. I pulled the car up to the delivery room entrance, jumped out of the car, and shouted, "Come quick. My wife is having a baby." Carmie laughed all the way to the delivery room, and I'm sure she is still laughing.

Upon Pat's birth, I went from the probability of never having a wife and child to having a beautiful family of five. Praise God! The next years were spent joyously raising our beautiful boys. We could never have imagined the terrible illness that lay before our loving and joyous family.

**The Brady Bunch**

# CHAPTER 5

# Two Months to Live

*1987*

In August of 1987, Carmie was working as a systems analyst at Prudential Property and Casualty Company in Holmdel, New Jersey. I was finishing up my studies to become a certified financial planner. She was now thirty-five years old, and we had been married for thirteen wonderful years. The boys were seven, five, and three years of age.

Carmie went to Dr. Dwyer for a routine physical. Upon completion of the exam, Dr. Dwyer said in a bewildered voice, "I feel something very unusual in your breast. I want you to have a mammogram. It may be nothing, but I don't want to take a chance."

The doctor who administered the mammogram read the X-rays and reported to Dr. Dwyer that Carmie had a fibrocystic disease that was nothing to worry about. At a subsequent visit, Dr. Dwyer still felt something that he did not like. He sent Carmie to a specialist.

The specialist examined Carmie and studied the X-ray. He then coldly told her, "Mrs. Brady, you have a rare form of cancer. It is called inflammatory breast cancer. It does not consist of a lump that can be removed. The cancer is made up of tiny cells that will metastasize if incised. The cancer is not operable. You are in the fourth stage of this cancer. You have two months to live."

Naturally, Carmie's body started to quiver. In her panic, she hoped that this "thickening" had only recently turned into cancer and that she had not had a malignancy for over four months. Crying uncontrollably, she proceeded to ask the doctor questions. "Is there any chance that you could be wrong?"

The doctor cold-heartedly held up his hand and said, "There is no sense asking me any questions. I can't help you. I am going on vacation tomorrow."

"Isn't there some way to treat this cancer?" Carmie pressed.

Then the doctor immediately squashed any hope she had. "What's the rush?" he asked sarcastically. "You've already had the tumor for four months."

Carmie prayed for the strength just to stand up from her chair. With her voice trembling and tears running down her face, Carmie asked, "Doctor, can I use your phone? I have to call my husband. You're telling me that I'm dying, and he doesn't even know I'm here."

The doctor replied, "Is it a local call?" Carmie left the office without making the call.

Carmie had planned to write a book about her experiences with doctors. I recently found some notes that she had made that give us an idea of her inner thoughts. Many of the quotes from the doctors in this book have been extracted from those notes.

Carmie wrote, "How my world had changed in just a few short moments. It's funny how one's perspective can change so quickly. When I arrived home, window awnings were being installed. I would have been absolutely thrilled to see those awnings up just the day before. Today, however, it seems so insignificant."

"A few minutes after I walked into the house, my son arrived home from his first day of nursery school, filled with joy and excitement. When I looked at him, my first thought was, *Oh my God, this is his first day of nursery school. Will I be alive to see him go to kindergarten?*"

I will never forget when Carmie came through the door and uncontrollably sobbed, "Chuck, I went to a specialist today. He told me that I have inoperable cancer. I have two months to live."

My heart sank. We cried together and hugged for a long time. I did not know what to say to her. Finally, I assured her that there would be another miracle. "Carmie, please don't despair! Please don't give up! God didn't keep you alive at Matt's birth for this. He will grant us another miracle."

Carmie replied with sudden strength in her voice, "I will live. My children need me." This was that strength and will to live for which Carmie has become a legend. "Chuck," she said to me, "I promised my mother that I would take her shopping. I can't let her down. What should I tell her?"

"Maybe you should say nothing until we have more information," I cautioned her. "Maybe the doctor is wrong."

Carmie bravely went out to the car to pick up her mother but quickly returned to get something she had forgotten. Thank God, the children were upstairs at this time. Carmie caught me screaming and crying, "God, please, please don't let her die. I need her. The boys need her. We can't live without her."

With inner strength and conviction, Carmie hugged me and said, "Chuck, I am going to beat this. I am going to live. I refuse to die. I have too much to live for. I have you and the boys. I will not let you down. God didn't keep me alive and give us three beautiful sons for this. I am going to live. I will not die. My children need me." Carmie then left to pick up her mother as promised.

At the time, I was working as a certified financial planner. I had promised Dan, a client, that I would stop at his house to pick up a check. As I entered his home, I became very emotional and burst out crying.

Dan asked, "Chuck, what's wrong?"

"Carmie has inoperable cancer," I cried, my voice trembling. "She has two months to live."

"Chuck," he replied calmly, "I can help you. For two years I've been seeing a spiritual healer. She has helped me immensely. My eyes were crooked in my head. I could hardly see. Now my eyes are perfect."

I believe very strongly that God has bestowed the gift of healing upon human beings. I wasn't sure, however, that Carmie would go to a spiritual healer. When I arrived home, I put my arms around her. We hugged and burst into tears.

"Carmie," I said, "Dan told me about a spiritual healer who has helped him. Why don't we go to her right away? Maybe God will grant us another miracle." We hugged again.

She laughed and said, "What can I lose? I have two months to live."

In her notes, Carmie had written: "Some doctors are spiritual healers who help to heal the patient both spiritually and physically, while other doctors lack empathy and do not have what people in the medical profession call 'bedside manner.' They do not seem to have any feeling for the human being on which they are working."

The following day, Carmie went to another doctor for a second opinion. "Maybe the first doctor was wrong," she said. "Maybe it isn't all that bad."

After the examination, the doctor calmly said to Carmie, "This is inflammatory breast cancer. The tumor is so large that it is inoperable." He went on crudely. "I can't cut that. Until recently, there was absolutely no treatment for this disease. Now, however, there are some new treatments; but quite frankly, I don't believe they will work."

Of this experience, Carmie wrote, "I felt like getting a shovel and digging a hole. If I had been shattered by the first doctor, all hope of survival was destroyed by the second."

# CHAPTER 6

# The Spiritual Healer

The following day we went to the spiritual healer. I believe that, just as Jesus gave power to the apostles to heal the lame, blind, and seriously ill people of His day, He chooses certain people and gives them the power to heal the sick in our day. The healer's name was Maria. She was one of the kindest, most empathetic persons I have ever met. Her understanding of human nature is unsurpassed by anyone I know.

Neither Carmie nor I had ever been to a healer, so we did not know what to expect. I was immediately relieved by the fact that the healing process did not involve a lot of mumbo jumbo where everyone cries and falls to the floor.

Maria took Carmie up to a room and had her lie down on a bed. The healer covered Carmie's eyes with a small towel and calmly laid hands on her. Prior to the healing, Carmie had been distraught, desperate, and physically exhausted. When Maria laid her hands on her, Carmie immediately felt heat emanating from her hands and relaxed completely.

Maria spoke softly to her. "Carmie, you must let go of the past. I feel that there is something in your past that is eating away at you. I feel that it is your father."

Carmie reluctantly divulged that there were some serious problems between herself and her biological father and between her mother and father.

The healer gently admonished, "You must rid yourself of any negativity that is in your mind and spirit. You

31

must forgive and let go of the past." She went on to say, "I feel beautiful love, kindness, and energy coming from your body and soul. I feel that you are going to overcome this disease and live a healthy life."

Carmie cooed in a soft, self-assured voice, "I know."

Maria later told me that the voice did not come from Carmie's lips or tongue. It came from deep down in her soul and heart. "I knew right away that Carmie was very close to God," Maria said, "and that she would be healed."

The very next day, as if by a miracle, we learned of two doctors who might be able to help us. For the first time, there was a slight glimmer of hope.

# CHAPTER 7

# Unnecessary Fear and Despair

On that same day, Carmie entered the hospital for the biopsy that had already been scheduled with the doctor who had given the second opinion. She lay in the bed with terrible trepidation for a very long time. The doctor who had told Carmie she only had two months to live never came to her bedside to explain the procedure.

When she returned to her room after the biopsy, she waited and waited for the doctor to come to her room to divulge the results of the biopsy. Finally the nurse in charge said to me, "You need to get her out of this hospital. I have seen too much. Take her to New York." Then the nurse paged the doctor, but he did not respond.

I went down to the commissary and saw the doctor, dressed in his operating garb, talking to someone. He looked over at me and continued with his conversation. I said nothing, because I thought he was in serious conversation about a patient's health.

I returned to Carmie's side. "Please get the doctor," she begged me. "I can't stand this. The doctor tells me I am going to die in two months and doesn't have the courtesy to tell me the results of the biopsy."

Once again, the nurse paged the doctor. A while later, the nurse came into the room and said with an embarrassed and disgusted voice, "The doctor is on the phone out in the hallway. He wants to talk to you."

I answered the phone. "Doctor, what is going on? Carmie has been lying here anxiously waiting for the results of the biopsy."

"She has inflammatory breast cancer," he responded. "Bring her to my office in the morning."

"Doctor," I replied, "I hope you don't mind, but tomorrow we are going to NYU and to Columbia Presbyterian Hospital to see two specialists for second opinions." To my astonishment, the doctor hung up the phone.

I went back into the room and told Carmie the bad news. In the trembling voice of someone who has just received a death sentence, she blurted out, "Please, go find the doctor. I have to talk to him." I went back down to the commissary where the doctor was again sipping coffee. When I interrupted him, he looked at me as if he did not know who I was.

I said, "Doctor, you just told my wife that she has two months to live. You are sitting here sipping coffee. You didn't even have the courtesy to tell her in person and give her some hope. What do we do now?"

Obviously, he was upset, not because of the results of the biopsy, but because we were going to New York for a second opinion. "Bring your wife to the office in the morning," he said to me tersely. Needless to say, we never went back to that doctor.

That evening Carmie returned home to the children. She laughed and laughed and played with the children as if nothing was wrong. She played with them until their bedtime and then tucked them into bed. Completely exhausted, Carmie and I went to bed and prayed. Carmie cried herself to sleep.

We arrived at NYU Hospital early the next morning. A young oncologist examined Carmie. She looked at the X-rays and spoke to us for about an hour and a half. She was very soft-spoken and empathetic. "I agree with the diagnosis. I am afraid that you do have inflammatory breast cancer." With sadness in her voice, she explained, "Mrs. Brady, this is one of the fastest moving cancers there is. There is not a doctor in NYU Hospital who will touch you. The cancer will metastasize when incised. The only thing I can offer you is an experimental program in which there is little chance that the medicine will work and a fifty percent chance that you will receive a placebo."

When we left the hospital, our bodies were drained. Our hopes and dreams had been shattered. There was no way that Carmie would accept a program that could result in her death.

# CHAPTER 8

# One Doctor Answers Our Prayers

We had to hang around in New York all day to see the doctor at Columbia Presbyterian Hospital. Carmie's good friend Judy, who was always there for us during this horrible stage in our lives, took us to lunch at a famous restaurant. We cried through lunch and then headed off to Columbia Presbyterian. When we arrived, we were informed that the doctor would be late, because he was coming from home just to see Carmie.

Five-thirty came and went. Finally, Carmie burst into tears. In utter despair, she sobbed, "That's it. I've had it. What's the sense? Everyone tells me that I am going to die." This was the first and last time that I ever saw Carmie give up hope. She was in the deepest moment of despair. She had fallen into a dark abyss. "Let's go home," she blurted. "Everyone is telling me that I am going to die. I give up."

Judy calmly and lovingly consoled her. "Come on, Carmie. Think of the boys. You must live for them. Please see this one last doctor."

"Carmie," I added, "please wait and see this doctor. God provided you with a doctor who saved your life when Matt was born. This could be the doctor whom He has sent to you now. This could be the beginning of another miracle."

Dr. Kister arrived at 6:00 p.m. He was a large, elderly man with what sounded like a Swedish accent. He was one of the kindest, gentlest people I have ever met in my life. He spoke to us for a while and then examined

Carmie. After checking the X-rays, he took Carmie by the hand. In the most empathetic tone imaginable, he said, "Mrs. Brady, I am sorry to tell you that you do have inflammatory breast cancer."

Carmie gulped and began to cry.

Dr. Kister squeezed her hand. "Mrs. Brady, I don't know who you have been talking to. As a child, I was twice before a Russian firing squad, and I am still here. Now I am an old man, and I am saving lives. I have a patient who has been alive for ten years with this type of cancer.

"I am going to keep you alive. If we keep you alive for ten years, there will be many new cures that we do not know about today. This is not going to be easy. We are going to take out all the ammunition—the tanks, the cannons, and the atom bombs. We are going to bombard you with chemotherapy. Together, we are going to beat this."

Carmie nodded and smiled. Her hope and faith had been renewed. The spirit of God had reached her through this one beautiful person.

"Mrs. Brady," the doctor added, "this is the fastest-moving cancer that we know of. We are going to use a very strong and fast-moving chemotherapy to combat it. Unfortunately, the chemicals will cause you to lose your hair within two weeks, and it will also cause you to gain weight."

Carmie laughed. "Great," she replied. "Not only do I have cancer, but I am going to lose my hair in two weeks and get fat." She shook her head and sadly laughed again. To Carmie, her hair was the most precious part of her body. When I first met her, she was going to Kenneth, Jackie Kennedy's hairdresser in New York City—and she was always on a diet. Now the doctor was telling her that she was going to be bald and fat.

"Mrs. Brady, please trust me," Dr. Kister pleaded. "Are you willing to go through hell to keep on living?"

"I'll do whatever you say, Doctor," she replied with renewed determination. "I want to live." Carmie looked at me and sobbed. "I *will* live. You and the boys need me. With the help of God, I am going to beat this! You and the boys and this good doctor and God will keep me alive."

Dr. Kister then said, "Carmie, I want you to meet Dr. Oster who is the oncologist who will administer the chemotherapy. Dr, Oster and I will work closely together. We will do everything in our power to defeat this terrible disease."

We immediately thanked Dr. Kister and, with renewed hope, proceeded to Dr. Oster's office. Dr. Oster had set his busy schedule aside and was waiting at the door of his office when we arrived. As soon as Dr. Oster began to speak, a feeling of peace and confidence came over us. We immediately knew that we had come to the right hospital and that we were in caring hands. As we left the hospital, Carmie uttered, "I love those doctors. I know that they are going to make me better." Little did we know that Dr. Oster would lovingly care for Carmie for almost twenty more years.

The following day, Carmie and I went looking for wigs. Unless you have been through it, you will never know what a traumatic experience it is. We went from store to store. With each wig she tried on, she became more depressed. The wigs looked like mops sitting on top of her head. "I can't stand this," she said. "Let's go." She cried all the way home.

The next day, we heard about a cancer survivor who had suffered through this horrible experience and was now in the wig business. As we entered her store, the woman immediately hugged Carmie. "Hi, Carmie. I know what you are going through. I have been through it myself." She studied Carmie's face and then helped her to find a wig. Finally, Carmie settled on one and purchased it.

Again, Carmie cried all the way home. "Chuck," she said, "I can't do this. I can't stand this."

"You can do it, Carmie. God will help you. Think of the boys."

Then she burst out laughing. "I can do it. I *will* do it… for you and the boys."

# Chapter 9

# Chemotherapy

Carmie's therapy was to consist of two weeks on the drugs doxorubicin (Andriamycin), cytoxin, and fluorouracil (5-FU). She was told that she would be on this regimen for one year and that she had a thirty percent chance of living for five years.

We walked into the chemotherapy room at Columbia Presbyterian Hospital not knowing what to expect. There are no words to describe the fear and trepidation that was in our hearts and souls. As we peered into the facility, we were terrified by the sight of two large rooms that contained reclining chairs all around the perimeters. In these chairs were some of the sickest people you could ever imagine. We saw children, teenagers, octogenarians, black, white, and Asian. Cancer is indiscriminate. It strikes at every family in all walks of life.

Carmie sat in a chair and we waited. It was then that we met an angel sent by God. Her name was Sue. From the beginning, it was obvious that Sue possessed an indescribable inner beauty that would manifest itself whenever she administered to Carmie. From that moment on, she was always there for Carmie. There was always a smile and a kind word on her lips. Carmie came to love Sue, and it was obvious that Sue loved Carmie. Just like doctor Kister, Susan would become Carmie's spiritual and physical healer.

On that first day of chemo, Sue placed her hand on Carmie's shoulder and smiled. "Carmie, you are my first patient. I am here just for you. If you need anything—water, soda, a kind word—if you feel any discomfort or pain or you simply want to talk, please call me."

Halfway through the therapy, Carmie smiled. "This isn't so bad," she said. "I can do this. I will do it for you and the boys."

Carmie had come to realize that the fear and anticipation of the treatments were far worse and more terrifying than the actual treatments themselves. She also came to realize that this room that had terrified her at first was not a room filled with hopelessness and despair. It was a room filled with hope and healing that was provided by the caring staff of Columbia Presbyterian Hospital.

# CHAPTER 10

# Spiritual Healings

Carmie continued to see Maria, the spiritual healer, each week and progressively felt more and more optimistic. During the healings, Carmie felt considerable heat emanating from Maria's hands. As the healings progressed, she became very aware of the intense heat in the breast that contained the cancer.

As we left one healing session, Carmie remarked in wonderment, "Chuck, not only did I feel intense heat in my breast, but I felt that there is a war going on inside of it. It's as if the healthy cells are attacking the sick cells and gobbling them up like Pac-Man."

Maria later told me that Carmie had done all of the right things. "She brought Dorothy and Bob and you and the boys to my house for healings. Not only did she receive healings here, but she continued to receive healings from her loved ones at home."

As a result of the healings, a warm feeling of peace and calmness overcame the fear and despair that was in Carmie's heart and soul. Despite the treatments and ravages of cancer, she was the most peaceful that she had ever been in her life. Almost from the beginning, there was a transformation in Carmie. She went from worrying about herself and about her own suffering, the pain, and the wigs, to reaching out and helping those sick people who were around her. It was as if the Holy Spirit came to her and took over her body and soul. She would calmly smile at her fellow patients and utter, "Don't despair! You can do it. God will help you."

Each person with whom she came into contact became a special friend. Her infectious laughter reached into the depths and souls of the sickest people you could ever imagine. There were times when, despite their illness, many people in the room, including the nurses, were laughing along with Carmie. She lit up the room. She was a cheerleader and an example to everyone. Each time Carmie walked into the room, eyes would light up, and people felt the joy of life through this beautiful creature of God. Carmie's fears and tribulations were changed and turned outward to those who could not cope with their own illness. "How are you doing? Keep your spirits up. We are going to make it together."

Carmie often prayed, "God, you kept me alive when I was supposed to die at Matthew's birth. You kept me alive for a reason. You can't let me die. You need me to help these people who are so sick and terrified."

Carmie and I were always in love, but now an unbreakable bond was quietly developing between us. There was a spiritual oneness that would increase and grow until the day she died. We were truly soul mates, living for each other and our children. Of course, we had our marital moments and arguments, but we did have a special relationship. I never missed a chemotherapy session. I had to be there for Carmie, and I knew that she needed me to be there.

Oftentimes, her wonderful friends would accompany us to the hospital. She would not have made it were it not for her friends, who were so kind, loving, and empathetic. Of course, there was Judy, who was always there for her. Then there was a caring group of friends who called themselves "the Juniors" because they had all been together in the Junior Women's Club many years earlier. Many of her good friends, including the Juniors, took turns accompanying her to New York. They prayed with her, played Scrabble with her, and celebrated her triumphs whenever she felt better or received good news. There was also Eileen, who on a moment's notice would join Carmie for a cup of coffee or a drink. They would laugh together when only laughter could make Carmie forget the fear and pain that enveloped her at the hospital and at home.

There are so many funny stories about Carmie and her friends. I wish I could relate all of them. Eileen often talks about the times she and Carmie went to the beach. "We would go to the beach no matter what the weather was like," Eileen said. "One time, the howling wind grew stronger and stronger. The sand was hitting us in the face like little pellets. Laughing hysterically, we turned our backs to the wind, put towels over our heads, and kept right on laughing."

The girls formed a bridge club. They would sit and talk and laugh for hours while playing only one or two hands. Eileen tells the story: "One day we were playing at Mary's house on the back porch. As it grew dark, the June bugs started attacking us. Loaded with bites, Carmie sat inside behind the screen door while the rest of us sat outside. Laughing, she continued to play through the screen. Within seconds, all of us were laughing so hard that we had to stop the game."

I am telling these stories because I am positive that the laughter invoked by Carmie's friends was as important as any medicine that was prescribed by the doctors.

I remember the time Carmie, Eileen, and Eileen's mother went to see the *Phil Donahue Show* in New York. His guest was the loveable comedian George Burns, who was nearing his one hundredth birthday. The boys and I watched the show on television. Carmie's infectious laugh attracted the attention of the cameraman, who kept zeroing in on her almost as much as he did on George Burns.

Carmie became known as the "Scrabble Nazi." No one could beat her. During the chemotherapy sessions, Carmie would laugh so hard at her victories over her friends that the nurses would start laughing—and then catch themselves and admonish her for laughing so loud. Denise, the daughter of one of her friends, called Carmie and begged, "Please, let my mom win one game. She comes home grouchy every time she plays Scrabble with you."

Columbia Presbyterian Hospital is in New York on the other side of the George Washington Bridge. We lived in Point Pleasant, which is in Central Jersey at the Jersey Shore. Normally it took us two hours to get to the hospital and two more to return home. During rush hour, the drive was even longer. Sandwiched between rides were the chemotherapy sessions.

By the time we returned to our home in Point Pleasant, we were totally exhausted. The boys would lovingly meet their mother at the door. Remember, the boys were only seven, five, and three years old. They knew that she was ill but did not know that she was seriously ill. As I look back, I think they knew more than we thought they did. Sometimes they would overhear us talking or would listen to our phone conversations.

"Mommy, Mommy, you're home!" they would say. "Are you feeling better?"

Carmie would lovingly hug and kiss each one of them and say, "Yes, I'm fine, but I need to lie down. Just give me an hour and then I'll play with you, and you can tell me all about school."

Carmie would lie down for an hour and then get up and insist on cooking dinner. After dinner she would play with the boys and listen to all of their stories about school and the other events of the day. She would laugh and play with them until she lovingly kissed them and tucked them into bed. Her unlimited love for them and their love for her motivated her to keep on fighting. Carmie and I did a lot with the boys. When she had a break in the chemo sessions, we took a trip to Niagara Falls to get our mind off of things and to bond with the boys.

**Brady Bunch at Botanical Gardens, Niagara Falls, Canada.**

Carmie and I would lie in bed and talk for hours. "Chuck, I'm tired, and I'm scared," she'd tell me.

"I know you are," I would answer her. "I'm scared, too. We must keep on praying. God has been good to us. Think about what He did for us when Matt was born."

"I know," she'd reply. "Matt and I were given little hope of living, and now we have a beautiful family of five.

We have to pray for another miracle." We talked over and over again about God and His infinite goodness, the miracle of Matt's birth, and our other two miracles, Scott and Pat.

We also had intimate conversations about suffering and pain and fear of death. Carmie would often say to me, "Chuck, put your hand on my head like you always do." I would put my hand on her forehead and pray for God's blessing and healing. We could actually feel electricity moving between our bodies and souls. Eventually, we would fall asleep out of sheer exhaustion.

Every two weeks Carmie went through the same seemingly intolerable cycle. There was the two-hour ride to and from New York and the three-hour, debilitating chemo sessions. Although she was receiving some of the strongest doses of chemicals, Carmie very seldom got sick to her stomach in the early stages of the treatments. I think it was mind over matter.

There were to be four months of these cycles. Through it all, Carmie kept praying and laughing. Her friends would come to the house to cheer her up and would soon be confiding in Carmie about their own problems. She consoled them as much as they consoled her. Her transformation continued. Despite her fear and tribulations, her faith in God was becoming more pronounced. She was developing a oneness with the Holy Spirit to whom she prayed so frequently.

As a result of all those days of fear and trepidation, I began to have pains in my heart. Dr. Kister recommended that I see Dr. Tenenbaum, whom he described as the leading cardiologist at the hospital. Once again, I met a doctor who was as much a spiritual healer as he was a physical healer. Little did I know that Dr. Tenenbaum would later save my life, not from heart trouble, but from a seriously perforated small intestine.

Dr. Tenenbaum's secretary Kathy was especially devoted to St. Therese. "Carmie," she said, "pray to St. Therese." She gave Carmie a statue of St. Therese and lovingly told us about the saint's life and love. St. Therese has inspired millions with her example of compassionate and selfless love for God and for her fellow man. Through sickness and darkness, she remained faithful, rooted in God's powerful love. St. Therese wrote, "My mission—to make God loved—will begin after my death. I will spend my heaven doing good on earth. I will let fall a shower of roses." Carmie and I immediately thought of the large, red rose that bloomed miraculously at the time Matt was born.

Carmie's love for me and the boys and her friends was boundless. She was constantly reaching out mentally and spiritually, making an indelible mark on everyone she touched with her love and courage. Through all of her fears and suffering, she was gradually becoming an instrument through which God was reaching out to those who needed His love and compassion.

During this entire time, a beautiful bond was noticeably developing between Carmie and her doctors and nurses. In mid-December, Dr. Kister called Carmie to his office. "I need to see you right away," he said.

When Carmie walked into the office, Dr. Kister put his arms around Carmie and hugged her. "Carmie," he told her, "the cancer is now operable. Mysteriously, all of the cells that were spread throughout the breast have come together into a single ball. Dr. Oster and I have confirmed it. You are going to live. We are going to do a radical mastectomy."

Carmie and I hugged and cried. We went out to dinner that night and celebrated with her mother and father and the boys. There were no thoughts of the pending operation.

Carmie's friends John and Chris threw a huge victory party. We celebrated as though she had already been healed. Throughout the night, Carmie's laughter permeated the room. "God has brought me this far," she rejoiced. "He won't let me down." We celebrated so hard that night that our friends Ray and Cherry had to load everyone who was at the party into their truck and drive us home.

As the day of the operation came closer, fear began to overtake us. What do people do who have no faith? We drew upon our faith in God and love for St. Therese and our Blessed Mother—and upon our love for our children and for each other. Always shining through the fear and anticipation was our hope and faith in God.

# Chapter 11

# The Operation

We arrived at the hospital early in the morning. Dr. Kister, who was waiting at the front door of the hospital, gave us each a hug and said, "This is it. This is the day we have been waiting for."

While Carmie was in the examining room, a nurse started to ask me questions. Name, address, etc. Then he asked, "What side is the cancer on?"

"Don't ask me that!" I exclaimed. "I would probably tell you the wrong side. Ask Carmie!"

When I told Carmie, she burst out laughing. Her laughter permeated the corridor of the hospital, and people came out of the rooms to see what was so funny. Here was a woman who was about to have a breast removed, laughing her heart out. Laughter cures! The nurses and doctors commented about how well Carmie looked. "She does not look like someone who has gone through months of chemotherapy. She looks perfectly healthy." It was as though she had already been healed.

That night, Dr. Kister sat at the foot of Carmie's bed for at least an hour. Although he probably never thought of it, he was truly a spiritual healer sent by God to cure this beautiful woman. The following morning, the nurses wheeled Carmie past me toward the operating room. I kissed her and blessed her. "God is with you." We held hands and prayed. I put my hand on her head as I had done every night. We felt that same electrical sensation that we had felt when she was wheeled out of the delivery room at Matt's birth. A feeling of peace and confidence came over us, and we knew that she was going to make it. This would be another miracle.

We were told that the operation would take about two or three hours. Three hours passed—then four hours, then five hours. I started to become terrified. I had lost all contact with the process. The only thing the nurses could tell me was that she was still in surgery. "God, please," I prayed. "What is happening? Please bless her. Please bring her back to me."

Finally, after what seemed like an eternity, I was told that Carmie was in the recovery room and that the operation was a success. I rejoiced and called her mother and father and her friends to share the great news. An hour later, they wheeled Carmie into her room. She was awake and resting comfortably. I would later learn that Carmie had the ability to withstand horrific pain and suffering. She smiled and even laughed a little. "I'm okay," she said. "It wasn't too bad."

The doctor walked into the room. He looked as if he had aged twenty years and was wiping his brow. His garments were dripping with sweat. He gave me an exhausted smile. "Doctor what happened?" I blurted. "What took so long?"

Dr. Kister wearily answered my question. "The cancer disappeared before my eyes," he said. "It turned into what I can only describe as hardened glue. Wherever the cancer had been, there was no cancer. I have never seen anything like this before. The glue-like substance was like cement that the scalpel could not penetrate. I literally had to chop off her breast and chop out the lymph nodes. It was as if a miracle had taken place before my very eyes."

I looked at Carmie. I was sure we were both thinking of Maria, the spiritual healer, and knew that God had granted us another miracle.

Christmas Eve was rapidly approaching. Carmie was insisting on being home for Christmas. Dr. Kister promised that he would do everything in his power to have her home with the children. Each night, after a long day's work, Dr. Kister would sit on Carmie's bed and encourage her to get well. His spiritual powers seemed to exceed his vast medical knowledge. He promised her that, if they could get the fever down, she would go home for Christmas. With a stern voice, she said, "Doctor, fever or no fever, I am going to be with my children on Christmas Eve!" On Christmas Eve morning, Dr. Kister came into the room and smiled. "Merry Christmas," he said. "Go home to the boys."

## Chapter 12

# Christmas Eve

When we arrived at Carmie's parents' home, they and our boys were waiting at the door. "Mommy, Mommy you're home! We love you. Are you all better?"

Carmie smiled from ear to ear. She looked absolutely beautiful. After all she had been through, she was radiant. Her face was beaming, her eyes sparkling. She was celebrating another miracle. She was laughing and crying at the same time. She was so energized by seeing her mother and father and the boys that she did not even lie down for a much-needed rest. She sat for hours, listening to the boys' stories about what had happened in school and in their lives.

That night, her mother cooked us a delicious fish dinner, as is the Italian custom. As weak as she was, Carmie sat at the table and laughed—and laughed some more. She was on the road to recovery. The sparkle in her eyes and the smile on her face openly revealed the love that was in her heart.

We took the boys home and put them to bed. Santa went back to Nana's house to get the toys and presents. On Christmas morning, the boys hugged and kissed their mom and then waited at the top of the stairs to make sure Santa had gone back up the chimney. Carmie was smiling from ear to ear. Her laughter could surely be heard on the other side of town. We were celebrating the birth of Jesus Christ and the rebirth of Carmie Brady.

After we opened presents, Carmie was exhausted and went back to bed. The boys helped me cook up a surprise for their mom—breakfast in bed, fit for a queen. Carefully balancing the trays outside her door, the boys sang Silent Night. Then they burst through the door. "Merry Christmas, Mommy! Merry Christmas, Daddy!"

Carmie and I cried tears of joy. Seeing us smiling and wiping away the tears, the boys laughed at both of us. We all laughed and ate breakfast off of Mommy's tray. We prayed together and sang "happy birthday" to Jesus. We then sang Jingle Bells and thanked God for the newest miracle.

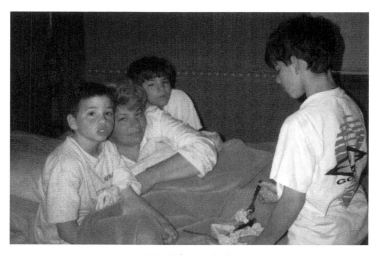

**Breakfast in bed**

# CHAPTER 13

# New Year's Eve

New Year's Eve approached. Our friends had planned to go to dinner to celebrate the new year. Carmie was unsure whether she would be strong enough to attend. Her friends, including the Juniors, begged her. "Carmie, please come—just for a little while."

Naturally, Carmie attended the party and stayed to the end. She laughed extra hard and loudly that night. It was the same laughter that had cured her in childbirth, the same laughter that had given her the strength to endure the horrible chemotherapy sessions, the same laughter that helped the cancer to turn to hardened glue. It was the same laughter that had allowed her to keep her hair and to live to celebrate a new year.

All of a sudden, an old man gruffly yelled from the other side of the room. "Come on, lady. Have a heart. Stop that laughing!" The room grew silent for a moment and, within seconds, most of the people in the restaurant began to cheer Carmie. "Keep on laughing! You're making our night!" Strangers even offered to send drinks to her, as had often happened when we went out to dinner. Little did they know that they were sharing in a miracle that was taking place before their eyes. That loud and infectious laughter was curing this beautiful woman. Other patrons were celebrating a new year. Carmie was celebrating a new life.

Everyone wanted to admonish the old man. We wanted to tell him that, only months ago, Carmie had been given just two months to live and that she'd had a radical mastectomy only two weeks earlier. Carmie pleaded with us. "Please don't say anything. That old man needs our love." As we left the restaurant, we all chimed in: "Have a happy new year. God bless you." The old man smiled and wished us a happy new year in return. Maybe Carmie's laughter had cured his loneliness.

One month later, Carmie had an appointment with Dr. Kister. He smiled and hugged her. "Carmie, you are cancer-free. You have been cured."

"But Doctor, don't I have to wait three years to know?" Carmie asked cautiously.

"You don't understand," Dr. Kister answered cheer-fully. "This case is different from any we've ever seen. You are cancer-free. Just to be safe, however, you will, have to undergo chemotherapy treatments for a year, and prob-ably four months of radiation treatments after that."

Carmie wept openly about the thought of undergo-ing treatments for another year, and yet she accepted the fact because she had to live for her children.


Two months later, we were in Dr. Oster's office, and he asked, "Carmie, do you remember when you were first in Dr. Kister's office that he told you the chemo-therapy would cause you to lose your hair in two weeks? The entire hospital staff is talking about you. We are all wondering…is that your real hair? Everyone tries differ-ent things, but nothing works. We were expecting you to lose your hair in two weeks. Are you doing something that is keeping your hair in?"

Carmie laughed. "Yes, Doctor, this is my hair. It is real. Every night before I go to bed, I pray real hard and then demand, 'Hair, stay in! Hair, stay in! Hair, stay in!'"

We all laughed.

The doctor smiled and said, "You probably talk to horses and dogs, too."

"Hey, Doc," I told him with laughter in my voice, "her hair stayed in. Maybe everyone should try it."

Dr. Oster chuckled. "I guess you're right," he said.

Just as the rose had bloomed on Matthew's birthday, Carmie never lost her hair. I believe this was yet another sign from God that another miracle had taken place.

# CHAPTER 14

# Miracle of Sight

## *1985*

Carmie had been the recipient of two miracles. Carmie and Matt are alive because of the miracle that took place at Matt's birth. At age thirty-five, Carmie was miraculously cured of cancer. Her faith in God and Maria, the spiritual healer, had grown to a point where she felt that her faith could move mountains. The reason that I have included Scott's miracle in this book is because I believe that it would not have happened were it not for Carmie's faith in God.

Scott had been born with *strabismus*, a condition commonly known as "cross-eyed." Whenever he looked down, his eyes crossed to his nose. When he looked up, they moved outward toward his ears. At the age of three, we took him to one of the leading ophthalmologists in the country. "I am sorry, Mr. and Mrs. Brady," he told us. "Scott will have to undergo a very serious operation in which the muscles of his eyes will be incised to bring them into line. Following the operation, Scott will feel terrible discomfort from what will feel like gravel in his eyes. The discomfort will last for only a few days."

We scheduled the operation for two weeks from that date. Following the operation, we sat and held the poor child on our laps until the discomfort and pain subsided.

One month later, we took Scott back to the doctor. He examined Scott and said, "I am very sorry, Mr. and Mrs. Brady, but the operation was only partially successful. Scott will have to wear glasses for the rest of his life." So Scott wore glasses that looked like the bottoms of Coke bottles. All the kids made fun of him.

When Scott was about four years of age, he was learning to ride a two-wheel bicycle. I had torn the calf of my left leg playing racquetball and was sitting on the front stoop with my leg in a cast. All of a sudden, the bike turned upside down, and Scott landed on his face. His glasses smashed. Blood gushed from his eye. I hobbled to him as fast as I possibly could and saw blood flowing profusely from his eye. I thought the glasses had cut his eye out. All I could do was cup my hand over the eye to stem the flow of blood. I hugged him. "You're okay, Scott. You're okay. You are going to be all right." When the ambulance arrived, we were relieved to find that the severe laceration was *above* his eye, not in it. The wound was surgically repaired, and Scott continued to wear his ugly glasses.

When he was five years old, Carmie came to me and said, "I am going to take Scott to Maria. She helped me. Maybe she can help him." When Scott returned from his session with Maria, we all had a good laugh. He looked as if he had been hit with a bolt of lightning. He staggered around, giggling and laughing, and then fell into a deep sleep. Maria told us that she had felt tremendous energy flowing through her body during the healing.

We continued to take Scott for healings. When he was about seven years old, Carmie noticed that, following a healing, his eyes were watering profusely. "Scott, are you all right?" she asked.

"Mommy, my eyes are sparkling," he replied. "I see sparkling lights in my eyes." Hoping for another miracle, we took him to the ophthalmologist, who said in amazement, "Mr. and Mrs. Brady, Scott's vision is 20/20.

He no longer has strabismus. He can throw the glasses away."

The next day we invited all of Scott's friends to a party. We covered the glasses with a towel, and Scott hammered them to pieces. We all cheered and praised God for yet another miracle.

Once again, Carmie's faith had been rewarded.

# CHAPTER 15

# Giving Back to God

Carmie had an excellent job with a well-known brokerage firm. One night she sat next to me and said, "Chuck, I need to talk to you. God has bestowed two miracles upon me. He has twice given me back my life when there was no hope. He saved me and Mathew and cured me of cancer for a reason. For a long time, I have been praying to God and St. Therese, and they have told me why I am alive. God wants me to help others, to share my experience, my fears and tribulations, my hopes and joys."

Carmie told me that she wanted to quit her job and go to work with the Ocean County Department of Social Services in order to get two years of experience in the field of mental health counseling. She then planned to enroll at Rutgers Graduate School of Education to get her master's degree in mental health counseling.

"God wants me to devote my life to people who are sick and in need of His help," she said.

Chills ran down my spine. I was so happy to hear her words. Her whole life has been devoted to helping others. Her laughter would help to cheer and cure those who were sad. Her love would transmit the love of Jesus Christ to those who were lonely. Her caring personality would bring the Holy Spirit into the souls of those who had little faith. With tears in my eyes and joy in my heart, I hugged her and said, "Carmie, God is calling you. This is why he kept you alive. He wants you to devote your life to helping those who are in need. Go for it. I am proud of you."

Carmie worked for two years in the Department of Social Services in the food stamps department. She delivered food stamps to the poor and downtrodden, pouring her heart and soul into her job. Much of her time was spent loving and encouraging her poor, unfortunate clients.

Carmie was immensely happy with her family life and with her chosen profession. In 1996 she enrolled in the graduate school at Rutgers University. She attended school during the day and studied and cared for her family at night.

In 1999 Carmie graduated cum laude with a master's degree in mental health counseling.

**Our proud graduate.**

Carmie took a position with Bayshore Counseling Center. Most of her clients were very poor and were suffering from mental health problems. She devoted the rest of her life to bringing the peace and love of God to those unfortunate people who were in such need of God's healing and love.

The years following Carmie's graduation and the years in which she worked at Bayshore Counseling Center were the happiest days of her life. Night after night, she would come home from work and say, "Chuck, I love my job. I am so happy."

I would be remiss if I did not mention Carmie's very happy and unusual home life during those years. Most parents have a hard time putting up with one or two teenagers living in their home. Carmie loved not only her sons but all of their friends. I cannot remember a day when there were fewer than ten teenagers in the house. When our sons' friends heard that I was writing a book about Carmie's life, they asked if they could write about some of the funny things that happened in the Brady household while they were growing up.

Scott's good friend Keith wrote:

> The Brady home was always filled with Matt, Pat, and Scott's friends. As teenagers, we went there after school or after sports. We often stayed there, studied there, and slept there. I don't know how Mrs. Brady put up with all of our friends. She must have loved us. We were always clowning around, wrestling and playing football in the house. I will always remember the two summers when I lived in the Brady's' house. Every morning we would wake up, and Mrs. Brady would have milk and bagels ready for us. She would sit and talk and listen and laugh for hours. Mrs. Brady was a beautiful woman who always opened up her heart and house to us.

Jonathan, another of Scott's friends, wrote:

> Although we lived with and loved our families, we felt as though we were also part of the Brady family. Growing up in the Brady home could not have been a better time in my life. I will always remember Mr. Brady's cooking, stories, and pranks. One night, we were climbing up the laundry chute to scare Mr. and Mrs. Brady. They let us get halfway up and poured a bucket of water on us. We ran away thinking that a pipe had burst.
>
> Who could forget Mrs. Brady's laughter when one of us made up a word trying to beat her at Scrabble? I will always remember her love and thoughtfulness.
>
> One day we were playing Hide and Seek. I was hiding in the attic when I fell through the floor and into the family room. Apparently, Mrs. Brady begged Mr. Brady not to yell at me or let on that he knew I'd done it. Only recently, after a few beers and a few of his stories, did he tell me that he knew I was the culprit.
>
> Then you have the Brady boys. To keep it short, I'll just say that we broke that house in pretty well with living-room football games and ransacking the refrigerator and pantry the second Mrs. Brady unpacked the groceries. Between her boys and their friends, there were always about ten teenage boys in that house, turning it upside down.

Carmie and I had recently redecorated the living room. It had become "Mrs. Brady's room," her little oasis in which she could sit and pray, meditate, and read in privacy. No one was allowed in it.

One day I walked into the house to find Jon standing in the hallway. He had just come in the house and was standing with his toes up against the threshold of the room. He lovingly said, "Hi, Mrs. Brady. You look beautiful. You dyed your hair."

Carmie let out a roar. She laughed so hard that tears were flowing from her eyes. Jon stood there with a bewildered look in his eyes and a smile on his face. Still laughing, Carmie blurted, "Jon. This is a new wig." Jon laughed, but he held his place at the entry to the living room until he heard the familiar words, "You can come in now."

Jon darted into the room and hugged and kissed Carmie. "I love you, Mrs. Brady. How are you feeling?"

My son Matt, knowing that his friends were contributing to the book, wrote the following:

> I think the best way to capture the essence of my mother is with a short story about her.
>
> I came home from work one day, and she was noticeably excited. She ran right up to me and said, "Matt, I have to tell you what happened today. I was in the supermarket, and I saw this extra-hot salsa, and I got it for you. I was so excited that one of the workers saw my face and asked why I was so happy about the salsa. I told him that my son loved spicy food."
>
> I do love spicy food, and since I was the only one in the family that did, I rarely got it at home. The mere thought of making her son happy with a jar of salsa got her so excited that a complete stranger asked her about it. This shows the type of person she was. No matter how big or small the

gesture, she always cared about making the ones she loved happy. That's what I miss most about her—her selfless, loving nature.

Matt's closest friend growing up was, and still is, Shawn Leonard. Shawn, who has always been like a son to me, is now a technical sergeant in the Air Force and a highly decorated war hero. I was proud to be present at the Pentagon when he received the highest award available in the U.S. Air Force for his heroism in Iraq and in Afghanistan. Shawn, whose plaque hangs in the Hall of Heroes in the Pentagon, wrote:

> Everyone talked about Mrs. Brady's laugh, because it was so unique and distinctive, so alive and so true. There was nothing fake about it. I remember the first time I was at the Brady house, which is on the water in Point Pleasant. I was sitting on the dock and heard a loud, full-of-life laugh coming from inside the house. I actually started to laugh to myself after hearing the sound. Soon after, Mrs. Brady came out, and I introduced myself. She was full of life, and there was this beautiful smile on her face.
>
> I think I stayed at the Brady's' house almost that whole summer—and many summers and winters thereafter. Mrs. Brady always treated me like I was one of her own; the whole family did. She made me feel so comfortable at their house. Everyone loved being at the Brady house.
>
> Over the years, the Bradys became like a second family to me. One time, Matt and I got back to the house really late, past curfew, and Matt was not feeling good because we had been drinking.

Mrs. Brady came out of her bedroom, stood at the top of the stairs, and started asking questions. She was very upset with us. Then Mr. Brady came out, and we knew we were in trouble. I tried to back my way out, but Mrs. Brady said, "Oh, no, Shawn, you're in trouble too. You are just as much to blame for being late as Matt."

Soon after that, Matt ran to the toilet and started to get sick. I went to the bathroom and heard Mr. and Mrs. Brady come downstairs. Not knowing what to do, I stood there with Matt's parents staring at me. Then I heard that incredible laugh. Even Mr. Brady was laughing as he took pictures of Matt throwing up in the toilet. We still got in trouble, but it was so funny to see her go from mad and upset to this incredible laughter.

The amazing thing about Mrs. Brady was that she never showed any pain to us all the years that she was sick. To be honest, I never knew how sick she was until after we graduated. All she showed was how to live, love, and laugh.

I love you, Mrs. Brady, and will never forget you. And—to Mr. Brady, Matt, Scott, and Pat—I can't thank you enough or show you how much you mean to me. I love you guys.

# CHAPTER 16

# Cancer Strikes Again

## *2000*

Life was good for the Brady bunch. Matt was a student at Mount St. Mary's College in Maryland, majoring in business management. Scott was a finance student at Loyola College in Maryland. Pat was a student at Point Pleasant High School and one of the best wrestlers in the state of New Jersey.

Carmie had been diagnosed as having fibroid tumors. As time passed, the tumors became enlarged, and she began to suffer terrible discomfort and pain. Dr. Dwyer decided that is was time to remove the tumors via a hysterectomy. The operation was supposed to be a routine hysterectomy with no complications. Because of all the other serious illnesses we'd endured, we kind of took this one lightly.

Prior to the operation, we hugged and prayed together. As we prayed, I pressed my hand upon her forehead. Once again, we felt the electricity passing between our bodies and souls. It was as if our souls were speaking to each other. Again I assured her, "You are going to be fine, Carmie. God will bless you as He has in the past. This will be an easy one. You will pass this test with flying colors. I love you."

Still thinking of others instead of herself, she responded in a soft and soothing voice. "I love you and the boys…my poor husband."

Once again, the operation took far longer than anticipated. Once again I spent many hours waiting and praying. "What could be wrong? God, please bless Carmie as you have in the past."

Finally Dr. Dwyer walked into the room. I looked into his eyes and knew that it was bad news. He took me into a private room and broke the news to me as gently as he possibly could. "Carmie's ovaries and the surrounding areas were filled with cancer," he said. "The cancer was hidden by the fibroid tumors." With tears in his eyes, he went on. "We did our best, but we could not get all of the cancer. There are still some cells remaining."

My heart sank. Chills went through my spine. "God, help us." I prayed silently. "How much more can one woman take? How much can she endure? Please, God, we need one more miracle."

Once again, we would return to Columbia Presbyterian Hospital for the dreaded chemotherapy sessions. The first chemotherapy session started off horribly. The experienced nurses could not find a vein into which to stick the needles. Carmie's veins had been destroyed by all of the previous piercings. She was jabbed over and over again by the endless line of nurses who deeply felt Carmie's pain and discomfort. Not one nurse could find a vein that was suitable to transport the medication into her body. My heart ached as I watched her wince in pain with each prick of a needle. As nurse after nurse apologized, Carmie simply smiled and softly said, "That's okay. I understand."

From out of the blue came a voice from heaven. "Carmie, what are you doing here?" Carmie smiled and breathed a sigh of relief. The voice was that of Sue, the angel God had sent to care for Carmie thirteen years earlier. Sue smiled. "Carmie," she said, "I haven't worked at this hospital for many years. This is my first day back. I will take care of you and help you to get better." Once again God was taking care of Carmie through this beloved nurse.

Sue picked up a needle and found the vein on the first try. She did not work in the chemotherapy area, but whenever Carmie needed to give blood or receive intravenous treatment, Sue would manage to be there for her. Through all this latest pain and anguish, Carmie would continue to laugh and love and cheer on her fellow patients.

Thirteen years of illness had taken their toll on Carmie. How could they not? This time she did lose her hair, and she became deathly ill after each chemotherapy treatment. She was constantly fatigued and often grew depressed, although she never showed it to her friends or clients. Now the rosary beads were always in her hand, the prayer to St. Therese always on her lips.

Her overwhelming faith in God and her love for St. Therese and our Blessed Mother drove her to new spiritual heights. Her love for her family and clients propelled her through her pain and self-pity and compelled her to infuse her laughter, love, and caring into the souls of those who tried to comfort her. With an everlasting love for people in need, she continued to drag herself out of bed each morning and to drive the forty minutes to the counseling center. "I love my job," she always said. "I love my clients. They need me. I cannot let them down."

Carmie's clients knew only that she was very ill. Even her best friends did not know that she was dying. She never once complained or looked for sympathy. She was always there for them. She never looked for pity. Day after long day, she listened to their problems, consoled and comforted them, laughed with them and cried with them. Through her ever-present faith and her love for God, she led them closer to physical and mental health and closer to her Lord, whom she loved so much. The following is a letter that she received from her successor after her health no longer permitted her to continue in her job.

> Dear Carmie,
>
> I just wanted to send you a note to let you know how much each and every one of your clients absolutely *adores* you. I've heard things like, "She's wonderful"; "She's so nurturing"; "I made great progress with her"; "She taught me so much"; "She really made a difference in my life"; "She helped me to accept my situation better"; and "She inspires me."
> Love,
> Janine

By now, Carmie's health had visibly deteriorated. In our hearts, we knew that she was nearing the end of her life. Until the day she died, Carmie's faithful friends would come to the house to pray with her, to share their love, to play Scrabble, and to make her laugh. I think her loving friend Eileen Mallon was one of the few people who realized how deathly sick Carmie really was. Day after day, she went with Carmie to the store, the movies, or to dinner; or they just sat and talked and laughed over a glass of wine.

Carmie was devastated when Eileen moved to Pittsburg. After she moved, her beautiful daughter Katie picked up right where Eileen had left off. She did all of the things her mother had done for Carmie. Eileen would later write, "Our children were the most important things to both of us. We spent so much time talking about them, worrying about them, and sharing questions and problems. Carmie was a wonderful listener and gave me great advice. I miss my best friend, but I know she is keeping an eye on me."

Carmie's friend Mary would sit and pray with her for hours and help her renew her spiritual strength and faith in God. Inevitably, as she conversed with her friends, they would forget about Carmie's problems. She would listen to their problems and console and counsel them as if she didn't have a care in the world. Through all of her problems, she continued to laugh, to love, and to care about me and the boys, her friends, and her clients. She received eternal strength through her spiritual healer and her love and devotion to the Holy Spirit, St. Therese, and the Blessed Mother.

Carmie was a beautiful person whose morals were surpassed by no one. She loved everyone and tried to help everyone with whom she came into contact. The faith for which she is now famous is not something that happened overnight. Through all of those years of suffering, I watched her grow in faith and love for God. Her faith grew day by day as she struggled to keep her promise: "I will live. My children need me."

Over and over, Carmie recited the rosary and prayed for strength and courage. Carmie did something that very few people in her condition would do. After her debilitated body would no longer allow her to drive to work, she gave her phone number to every client. Until the day she died, she would receive phone calls at all hours of the day and night from people who were crying out for mental and spiritual help.

Day after day, night after night, she would receive phone calls from former clients who needed to feel her love. They needed to hear her voice, because she loved them so much. They needed to hear her laughter, because it lifted them up to greater heights. Over and over, I heard her answer the phone at all hours of the night and day: "Hi. I'm so glad you called. No, that's all right. What's wrong? Please tell me how I can help you."

Listen to the words written to her by one of her clients:

> You have made the biggest impact on my life, and I want to thank you from the bottom of my heart. I know that you would say that it is your job, but you didn't make it seem like that to me. You really cared about helping me, and it showed in the progress I made. You have a great laugh. Keep it up. Prayer is very good. You taught me that. When problems arrive, I keep telling myself, "I survived this before, and I'll survive it again." A very sweet, funny, and caring person taught me that—*you*. God bless you and keep you safe. I really do miss you. Everyone does.

# CHAPTER 17

# The End Is Near

### *2004*

Four years passed after Carmie was operated on for ovarian cancer. Time and time again, the doctors called her into their offices to tell her that she had gone into remission. Each time, the doctors expressed shock—not only about the fact that she kept going into remission but about her vibrancy and utter strength of character and mind.

Carmie's time had not yet come. Jesus wanted her to continue bringing His love and caring to all with whom she came into contact. He must have wanted her contagious laughter to ring out for a few more years. Throughout the life that she cherished, we could see that she was not done sharing, laughing, loving, and caring.

I hate to be crude, but what I am about to write is very important in understanding how sick Carmie was. One day when I came home from work, Carmie's wonderful friend Linda was sitting at her feet, holding her hand. Right away, I knew something was terribly wrong. Carmie sobbed, "Chuck, my intestines are emptying through my vagina. It's disgusting." My heart sank to depths that I could never have imagined. In my heart, I knew this was the beginning of the end, and I could sense that she felt the same.

The doctors scheduled a colostomy for the following week. What did Carmie do? Three days in a row, —even knowing that the end was near—she put on a maxi pad and went to lunch with each of her three groups of friends. Her friends later told me that they did not realize how sick she was because she laughed throughout the meals.

**Healing with friends**

Carmie never let her friends know how sick she was, nor did she let them know of her discomfort. Throughout lunch, she laughed and laughed and shared her love and caring spirit with her best friends.

Two days before the colostomy was to take place, Carmie became seriously ill. I didn't think she would make it through the night. I called her surgeon in New York, who told me to bring her in right away. I called the Point Pleasant first-aid squad, who couldn't have been more caring. With hearts filled with sorrow, they informed me that they could not drive her to New York. It was against the law.

They helped me and my son Pat carry her limp body and place her in the back of the car. As they lifted her in, they almost dropped her. Even though she was in excruciating pain, she burst out laughing. "Thank you for being so kind to me," she told them. "God bless you." They covered her with blankets, and she smiled at them and thanked them again.

Pat drove us to New York. God bless Pat. He had suffered so much with his mother. When Carmie and I were admitted into the emergency room, Pat was forced to sit in the waiting room of the hospital. This was in Washington Heights, which is called the "drug capital" of New York. It was one of the most horrible scenes anyone could imagine. If I had been waiting there, I would still be having nightmares. As soon as I could, I told Pat to go home. There was nothing that he could do at the hospital. "Go home and pray for mom," I said.

The wonderful staff at Columbia Presbyterian Hospital took Carmie in their arms and cared for her. I stayed by Carmie's side all night as she was prepared for the operation. "God, please help her. Please don't let her suffer." My prayers were different now. The electricity was still flowing between our bodies and souls, but my prayers were more subdued and more accepting of God's will. No longer was I praying, "Please don't let her die." Now I was begging, "Please don't let her suffer."

Following the operation, Carmie was placed in a private room. The hospital nurses knew that I would not leave her side, so they arranged for me to have an adjoining room free of charge. God bless the staff at Columbia Presbyterian Hospital. They treat every person as if he or she is a member of their own family.

The following day, Carmie was in terrible pain. We waited in anguish for the colonoscopy specialist to show Carmie what was needed to care for herself. Carmie looked at the bag in disgust. "I can't do this. I can't do this," she said.

I prayed all day. "God, please give her the strength to endure this humiliating and nauseating debilitation. St. Therese, she loves you so much. Please help her."

I watched as the nurse showed her how the bag worked and how and when to empty it. I looked on in pity and said to myself, "She will never accept this. Dear Lord, please help her to overcome this new obstacle." I dreaded seeing the nurse leave the room, because I knew that Carmie was going to fall apart. I didn't know how to handle this new crisis.

When the nurse left the room, Carmie looked at me with tears in her eyes. But then she burst out laughing. "I can do this," she said. "This isn't the end of the world. With the help of God, I can and will do this. I will do it for you and the boys."

A few days later, Carmie sternly addressed Dr. Oster. "My son is graduating from Loyola College in Baltimore. I am going to go to the graduation no matter what you or anyone else has to say."

The doctor smiled lovingly. "I'm sorry, Carmie," he replied, "but that is out of the question. You are a very sick person. You are extremely weak from the operation. You have an infection and are running a high fever."

Once again, Carmie sternly replied, "Doctor, get me out of this hospital. I am going to my son's graduation even if I have to sign myself out."

By now, Dr. Oster knew of Carmie's strength and determination. He knew of her great courage and ability to overcome all obstacles. He simply smiled and said, "We will do what we can." In his heart, I'm sure he knew that she was going to the graduation.

# CHAPTER 18

# Scott's Graduation

## *2000*

A few days after Carmie returned home, Pat and I carried her weak and broken body to the car. As we lowered her into the backseat, she screamed in pain. The morphine gave her no relief whatsoever. Pat and I pleaded with her. "Mom," Pat begged, "please don't go. You are in terrible pain."

Only as I was completing this book, did Pat remind me of Carmie's response. Pat said to me, "Dad, all I ever cared about was wrestling. When I took third in the National Championship as a sophomore, I was determined to win the nationals the following year. I didn't care whether I graduated from college or not. What Mom said to me in that car changed my mind and my life."

Mom said, "Patrick, the most wonderful thing a mother can do in her life is see her son graduate from college. I'm not getting out of this car. I'm going to see Scott graduate."

Pat continued to share his inner thoughts with me, "At that moment I made the decision to quit wrestling and to study as hard as I worked at wrestling. I would graduate from college and make Mom happy and proud of me."

Pat graduated from The College of New Jersey in 2007 and is now a teacher and Head wrestling coach at his alma mater, Pt. Pleasant High School.

Summoning all the courage and strength she had left, Carmie reached up, grabbed onto the handrail of the car and proclaimed, "I am not getting out of this car. I am going to see Scott graduate."

The trip to Baltimore was one of the longest and most agonizing trips one could imagine. Each bump and turn brought cries and moans from her stricken body. With each bump and moan, Pat would ask, "Mom, are you all right?"

"I'm fine," she would answer. "Keep driving. I can do this. I am going to see Scott graduate." All the way to Baltimore, she prayed the rosary and begged St. Therese to give her strength.

When we arrived at the hotel, we were perplexed as to how we would get her out of the car. Matt met us at the door of the hotel. He and Pat took the wheelchair out of the trunk and placed it beside the open door. To our amazement, Carmie jumped out of the car and into the wheel chair. She smiled and uttered, "Thank God, we're here. I can't wait to see Scott." The thought of seeing Scott and attending his graduation completely blocked out the physical pain and suffering.

That evening, we all shared our love over dinner in the hotel room. Over and over, the boys told their favorite stories about the wonderful times that we'd had together as the Brady bunch. I must confess that Carmie and I had never heard some of those stories before that night. Through all of her pain and suffering, Carmie laughed and laughed for many hours. I think we all felt deep in our hearts that we were partaking in our last supper.

The following day, we took Carmie to the graduation. She sat in the wheelchair, looking for Scott in the dense crowd of graduates. Her love for Scott and her pride in his achievement made her oblivious to the pain that enveloped her body. The boys and I were unable to pick Scott out in the crowd. With a burst of pride and jubilation, Carmie blurted out, "Look! I see him. There he is, over there." She smiled from ear to ear. "I am so proud. Thank God I made it." She stayed to the very end of the graduation. The heavenly smile never left her face.

Once again we ate dinner in the room. She laughed as we recalled again the wonderful love that we shared as a family. We took what would be our last pictures together. Somehow, without my knowing, she managed to speak to each boy individually. She was preparing them for "life after Mom."

I now realize that whatever words she shared with them made an indelible imprint on their lives and souls. I never asked the boys what she said to them, but I know those words will stay with them for the rest of their lives. They are imprints of their mom's love that will always remain in their hearts.

The boys went out to celebrate Scott's graduation. Carmie and I passed the night together in the room. No longer did we talk about overcoming death. We held hands and counted the blessings that God had bestowed upon our lives. We passed the hours speaking proudly about the boys and what wonderful young men they had become. As she dozed off, she smiled. From the depths of her heart and soul, she sighed, "We did a good job! We did a good job. We did a good job." As she slept, I kept my hand on her head. Once again I felt the electricity, and I prayed, "Your will be done. Please, Lord, don't let her suffer."

When we arrived home after a long and tedious drive, we carried Carmie into the house and placed her onto the bed that the boys had placed in the living room. She had made herself live to be present at Scott's graduation, and now she was ready to let herself go and pass on to the new life that God had prepared for her. I would miss her terribly, but deep in my heart, I knew it was time for God to take his favorite rose from a life of suffering and pain to her eternal resting place.

## CHAPTER 19

# God Is Calling

That night Carmie was rushed in an ambulance to the nearby hospital. When I arrived at the emergency room, I immediately noticed that the doctors were working frantically over her. After more than an hour, a nurse came to me and said, "It was close. We almost lost her."

A doctor explained to me that Carmie had gone into cardiac arrest and was in shock from sepsis. Her heartbeat had dropped to zero, and her kidneys were failing. I will always remember one beautiful nurse who worked way beyond her shift to minister to her.

Soon Carmie was moved into the critical care unit. As soon as I laid eyes on her, I knew that the end was near. She had tubes going into her arms, legs and throat and an oxygen mask on her face. I placed my hand on her head and prayed as I had done so many times. I still felt the same electricity, but this time my prayers had changed. I was praying for a different miracle. "God, your will be done. Please take her home to everlasting peace and happiness. Your will be done."

I went into the waiting room and called the boys at home. "Mom is dying," I said. "Please come over."

Pat had already been through so much, he could not stand to see his mom suffering anymore. "Dad is it okay if I stay home and pray for Mom?" he asked.

I sighed. "Please stay home, Pat. Mom will understand."

I called Dr. Dwyer, the doctor who had saved her life in childbirth. He rushed to the hospital and sat with me

87

and the boys and a doctor whom Dr. Dwyer introduced as the head of the critical care unit. Dr. Dwyer explained the seriousness of the situation and told us that he felt it was time to let Mom go to her eternal rest. He turned to the other doctor. "Don't you agree?" The other doctor nodded his head in agreement.

Dr. Dwyer recommended that I call Dr. Oster, Carmie's oncologist at Columbia Presbyterian hospital. In his loving and empathetic voice, Dr. Oster told me, "Mr. Brady, it's time to let her go, there is nothing that can be done. Her insides are completely destroyed."

I replied, "The doctors here are insisting on trying a new procedure on her."

He responded emphatically. "Don't let them do it. Tell them to call me right away. I will fax her records to them and confer with them about her medical history." I found out later that the doctors never contacted Dr. Oster or the surgeon who had operated on her. From the very beginning of this crisis, Dr. Dwyer confirmed that it was time to let her go to God.

I presented the doctors with Carmie's living will and medical power of attorney, which specifically stated that they were to take no extraordinary measures to keep her alive. They were instructed to make her comfortable. I specifically instructed them: "My wife does not want to suffer anymore. She has great faith and is ready to go to God whom she loves so very much."

I went back into the room and prayed with Carmie. Throughout the day, I contacted each of Carmie's closet friends and told them of Carmie's condition. At first, I asked them not to visit her, because I didn't want to upset her. When I realized that the end was near, I called her friends and told them they could visit her for the last time.

About thirty of her friends, made up of three separate groups of men and women, stood outside of the critical care unit. Present were the ever-faithful "Juniors" about whom I have previously spoken. There were friends from all over Point Pleasant who loved her dearly, and there was a group from Brielle whom she had met through her wonderful friend Judy. Carmie was the beacon who brought everyone together. She was the glue who held them together.

These were the traits that her good friend Beth later wrote about: "Carmie really showed us all how to live and laugh and love. When the Brady bunch gathered in her kitchen, you realized what a diverse group of friends she had collected. Like the colorful patchwork quilts she made, we were held together by a strong, common thread: Carmie Brady."

Carmie was doing in death what she had done in her life. She was uniting people from all walks of life into one common thread. The nurse who was on duty at the time was absolutely wonderful. She realized that each friend needed to tell Carmie that he or she loved her and to say good-bye. The nurse allowed two people at a time to go into Carmie's room to share their unending love for the last time. Carmie did not speak. She simply looked into their eyes. Her eyes said to each of them, "I love you."

When everyone had left, Scott said, "Dad, I have to see Mom." Scott and I went into her room, and Scott blurted out, "Mom, I'm sorry."

Dr. Dwyer had come into the room behind us and immediately admonished him. "Young man, don't blame yourself. Your mom lived to see you graduate. That's why she went to your graduation. She would have it no other way. She has fulfilled her dream."

Each of the boys kissed her and said, "Mom, it's okay. You can let yourself go to God. We'll take care of Dad and Nana." We recited the "Our Father" prayer together and left for home with heavy hearts. There were four of us in the house, but it seemed so empty. This was a foretaste of what was to come without Carmie's loving presence in our home.

At 10:30 p.m. on May eighteenth, I received a phone call from a surgeon. He told me that he needed me to come to the hospital immediately to sign some papers. Shaking from limb to limb, I rushed to the hospital. The doctor was waiting for me with official papers in his hand. He informed me that he was going to operate on Carmie in the morning and that he needed me to sign a release.

I looked at him in utter astonishment and retorted, "Like hell you are. Doctor, did you take the time to call Dr. Oster?"

"Who is Dr. Oster?" he asked.

I'm embarrassed to admit that I absolutely lost it. As I write these words, my hands are trembling. "Doctor," I said, "you are going to operate on my wife, and yet you admit that you know nothing about her medical history? When you went into her room just now, what did you do? Why did she scream and cry out?"

The doctor told me that he had noticed the terrible edema in her hip; she was so full of infection that her skin was about to burst open. He said that he had simply touched her hip, and she screamed out in pain. He planned to cut from one end of the hip to the other to release the infection and relieve the pain. Following that procedure, he would perform an exploratory operation in order to repair her insides. It was obvious that he knew absolutely nothing about Carmie's medical condition, nothing about the years of treatment, nothing about the suffering and pain that she was going through, nothing about the colostomy, nothing about Dr. Oster's conclusions.

"It is time to let her go," I demanded. "There is nothing more that can be done." I was now in a very emotional state of mind. I proceeded to inform him of her complete history. I cried out, "I presented the doctors with Carmie's final directive and medical power of attorney. I instructed them to withhold all extraordinary measures, and you tell me that you are going to operate on something that is not operable. It is my final decision and Carmie's final decision to stop interfering with the will of God."

After hearing about Carmie's medical history, the doctor could not have been any kinder or more understanding. With great empathy, he sighed and replied, "I fully agree with you. I will meet with the staff early in the morning, and we will stop all medications except for those that will make her comfortable."

The following morning I returned to the hospital at 6:30 a.m., expecting to meet with the surgeon and the other doctors. The first person I met was the wonderful nurse who had been so kind to us the night before. She wished me "Good morning" and cheerfully stated, "Your wife has the most infectious laugh." Even in dying, Carmie was bringing joy to those who were caring for her.

I then met with the doctor who was on duty and that same nurse. I repeated what Dr. Oster had said and stated that the surgeon to whom I had spoken last night had agreed. "There is no procedure or operation that can repair the damage that has been done," I said. "It is time to let her go."

"That is all well and good," the doctor replied, "but I plan on trying a new procedure." In all fairness to the doctor, I can only assume that he wanted to do all in his power to save Carmie.

The nurse cut him off. "Doctor, this woman is in complete breakthrough. Even the strongest doses of medicine cannot ease her pain. She is suffering horribly."

Once again I invoked Carmie's living will. The doctor humbly and kindly agreed to move Carmie to the cancer ward where she would be made as comfortable as possible as she awaited her passage into eternal life.

That afternoon, Carmie was moved to the cancer section of the hospital. The nurses in the cancer ward were angels of God. It was as if they too felt the terrible pain that Carmie was going through as they lifted her from the gurney onto her final resting place on earth. I will never forget the kindness and empathy that the nurses bestowed upon me and Carmie during those last hours. Although she did not speak, Carmie was awake and following my every word. Her heavy breathing had slowed to a peaceful sigh.

I will never forget the look of peace and tranquility that was in her eyes as I spoke. "Carmie, I love you, and I will miss you terribly. The boys and your mother love you. We will miss you, but it's time to stop suffering. God and St. Therese are waiting for you. St. Therese is waiting for you with a big red rose just like the one that bloomed on Matt's birthday. Jesus is waiting with His arms outstretched. He loves you and wants to hug you. I will take care of the boys and your mother, and they will take care of me."

Carmie sighed and once more whispered to me about our wonderful sons. Just as she did on the night of Scott's graduation, she whispered from the depths of her soul: "We did a good job. We did a good job. We did a good job." I knew that they were the last words I would ever hear from her. "We did a good job." I will take her words with me to my grave.

I vividly remembered that, when Carmie's loving stepfather, Bob, had been dying, Matt and Scott had stayed with him throughout the night. The following day, Carmie had called the boys and suggested that they leave the room so that Bob could let himself go in peace. As soon as they left the room, Bob let himself pass into eternal life.

I reminded Carmie's mother about Bob's death and about Carmie's wishes. I suggested that we say a prayer and leave the room so that she could let herself go to Jesus in peace. Carmie's mother, remembering how Bob had waited for the boys to leave the room, agreed with me. I kissed Carmie and said, "Go in peace. I will love you forever." I will always remember the look of love and resignation that was in her eyes. She was ready to embrace God's love. With an empty heart, I left the room so that she could pass on to a greater life and love.

# CHAPTER 20

# Life Is Not Ended but Merely Changed

*May 21, 2004*

I had suggested that the boys go out with their friends to pass the time. I was sitting home by myself when the phone rang. It was that wonderful nurse who had been so empathetic. "Mr. Brady, I'm sorry. Your wife has passed away. Would you and the boys like to come see her?"

"No, thank you," I responded. "We want to remember Carmie as she was. I will spend the night with the boys, reminiscing about the wonderful life that we had together." I called the boys on their cell phones. "Mom is now with God and Poppy. She will never again suffer. Please come home."

The three boys arrived home at the same time. We stood together on the front porch and hugged and cried our hearts out. All of a sudden, Pat—who had suffered the brunt of his mom's ordeal because he was living at home during all of her suffering—blurted out in a strong voice, "Dad, Mom doesn't want to see us like this. She wants us to celebrate her life, not mourn her death. You get the cigars, and we'll make the drinks. We'll sit in the yard and talk about the great times we had with Mom."

In one of the greatest signs of faith that a family could have, we sat in the backyard and celebrated Carmie's life. We sat until four in the morning, talking over good times. I don't know what the neighbors thought. Our mom and wife had just died, and we were laughing hysterically about our lives together as a family. We reminisced about the wonderful trips that we had taken. We laughed about the great times we'd had with Nana and Poppy and about the parties that the boys had while Carmie and I were away. We must have talked about a hundred incidents that had taken place during our wonderful lives as the Brady bunch.

Over and over we thanked God for our wonderful mom and wife and the wonderful family that He had bestowed upon us. "Dad," Scott commented, "God has truly blessed us. We were not even going to be a family. Mom and Matt were supposed to die at Matt's birth. Had it not been for God's miracle, we would not even be here."

We celebrated Carmie's life and death that night. There would be no more suffering. Mom was at peace with God, our Blessed Mother, and St. Therese whom she loved so much. We felt Carmie laughing right along with us. We felt her caring presence and her everlasting love. We knew in our hearts that her laughter would ring out forever.

The following morning, Matt did what I could not do. He called each one of our relatives and friends and informed them of Carmie's passing.

# Chapter 21

# I Will Always Be with You

Carmie loved the beach and the sound of the ocean. Whenever she wanted to be close to God, she sat in one particular spot on the beach and was at one with God. The morning after Carmie died, her loving and sorrowful friends held a prayer service at Carmie's favorite spot on the beach. They stood in the sand with tears in their eyes and reminisced about the joyous life of their now-departed friend.

They spoke of the undying love that she had for all of them and everyone with whom she came into contact. Even in their hour of sorrow, they felt her love and heard her boisterous laughter. With tears in their eyes, they each said a few words and prayed for Carmie. Each person held a balloon.

**Carmie's friends say goodbye**

When they finished praying, they let go of the balloons and watched them swiftly rise up into the air and off to the south as if they were soaring into heaven with God's new saint. Carmie's friends milled around and reminisced about the wonderful life that they had shared with her. The balloons were soon out of sight. With tears in their eyes, her grieving friends turned to leave the beach.

All of a sudden someone yelled, "Look, the balloons are coming back." The balloons returned and hovered over the friends Carmie had loved so much. It was as if she was telling them: "Do not grieve or leave in sorrow. My departure is only temporary. I will always be with you—laughing, loving, and caring for you as I did in my life on earth."

I sincerely believe that the return of the balloons was a precursor of the many miracles that have taken place since Carmie passed into eternal life.

# Chapter 22

# The Viewing

The boys and I spent that morning picking out pictures of their mom for the funeral parlor. Each picture brought back wonderful memories of our beautiful wife and mom. Our conversation was filled with comments like these: "Look, here is a picture of Mom at Matt's christening. Here's a picture of Scott smashing his glasses after his eyes were miraculously healed. Here she is at the victory party thrown by her friends when she learned that she had been completely cured of cancer. Here's Mom with Nanny and Poppy on the sailboat. Here's one of Mom hiding her eyes at Pat's wrestling match. Mom is still here with us. She still cares for us and loves us. We can still hear her laughter and feel her everlasting love. She will care for us for the rest of our lives."

The hours leading up to the viewing were very tense. We had begun thinking more about Carmie's death and suffering. How would we get through the day? What would we say to her relatives and friends? What would they say to us? Even the weather report was bleak. Severe thunderstorms and dangerous winds were forecast. People had been warned to remain inside. When the time finally came, the boys and I knelt and said a prayer in front of Carmie, then stepped off to the side to witness one of the greatest outpourings of love that one could ever imagine.

Our fears and trepidation were immediately turned to gratitude and love. Within a few minutes, the two large rooms in the funeral parlor filled up with Carmie's relatives and friends. When we saw all those who had come, we were immediately consoled and were once again at peace with Carmie's passage into her new life. Over and over again, we hugged the mourners and consoled them.

As we hugged, I comforted people. "Carmie was supposed to die at Matt's birth. She was given two months to live when she was diagnosed with breast cancer almost twenty years ago. We have been blessed by God to have had Carmie in our lives for so many years. God blessed us with a beautiful wife and mother, and now He has called her from her intense suffering to a life of love and peace."

Tears of sorrow turned to tears of love and joy. Sighs of grief turned to sighs of relief and resignation. I said to the boys, "Mom was blessed in death as she was in her life." As the lines grew longer, the sky grew darker and more ominous. The line of mourners and well-wishers snaked through the entire first floor, out the door, around the huge parking lot, and down the sidewalk. The police department called for extra men to manage the traffic.

What a beautiful tribute to this wonderful child of God! There had to be over a thousand mourners waiting in line. Each mourner waited to tell us his or her story about how much Carmie had done for them. Two women came up to me on separate occasions and said, "I did not know Carmie, but I heard so much about her strength and how much she had helped people, I had to come and pay my respects." Many of her clients came and thanked us for sharing Carmie's love with them. All of them praised Carmie for her love and compassion. Of course, they also rejoiced in her laughter.

The storm passed us by. Once again the Lord watched over Carmie and her loved ones. After the viewing, the boys each spoke with amazement. "Dad, everyone came up to us with gloom in their eyes and sadness in their voices. We were the ones doing the consoling. It was as if we were healing their hearts and souls."

# CHAPTER 23

# The Mass of Resurrection

People came from far and wide to pay their final respects. The church was packed to the rafters. Members of Pipes and Drums of the Jersey Shore greeted us at the door with their beautiful music. Several priest friends of mine concelebrated the Mass. Father Maurice Carlton preached the sermon.

Father Moe, as we affectionately call him, is a huge man, about 6'3" and 280 pounds. He pointed to himself and said, "I always considered myself to be a tough man." He pointed to Carmie and said, "You want to see tough? *That's* tough. Carmie was the strongest, toughest, and most loving person I have ever met." He then pointed to my sons. "You think you wrestlers are tough? You think Navy SEALs are tough?" Once again, he pointed to Carmie and said, "*That's* tough." He spoke about how often Carmie had put her suffering aside in order to help and console others.

### Matt's Eulogy

Whenever I have done any sort of public speaking, I have always had the same problem. I could never figure out how to start. But with my mom it was easy, because how could you talk about my mom without talking about her laugh—that loud, amazing, sometimes embarrassing, and infectious laugh? I remember one time when my family and I went out in the boat to watch fireworks. The show was about to start, and it was pitch-black out. My mom started laughing, and out of the darkness someone yelled, "Carmie, is that you?" It was a boatload of her friends who recognized her by her laugh. By the time the fireworks started, there were five boats—each filled with her friends—tied to our boat. Her laugh was the beacon.

That's the way it always was with my mom. Look around at each other. Think about how many of you are friends because my mom brought you together. A lot of you may not know this, but my mom was a great beer-pong player. At my twenty-first birthday party, my friend and I were running the table when an easy win approached—my mom and my youngest brother, Pat. Well, before we knew it, we were down five cups. This was my youngest brother and my mom, and they were tearing us up in front of all of my friends. It was not the best birthday present.

People always ask me, "Who's the toughest Brady?" They always look at me and my brothers first and then settle on my dad. But they miss the one who was truly the strongest. They miss the one who, time and time again, faced insurmountable odds and came out on top. So, for once and for all, the answer to the toughness question is—my mom.

I want to tell you two stories that truly exemplify what my mom was about. The first time she had cancer, she was told she had just weeks to live. She went to the mall and was sitting on a bench, thinking to herself, "I am going to die. These people are just walking by me. No one knows it, but I am going to die." What she took away from this was a lesson she always taught the rest of us. "You never know what someone

104

else is going through," she told us. "When you deal with people in your life, you don't know what's in their heads, so take that into consideration when you are out there in the world."

The second story I want to tell you is about the day me and my brothers and a few of our friends were sitting around, just hanging out. My mom came in, and we were all joking around, when all of a sudden my mom decided to teach us all a lesson. Out of nowhere, she looked at all of us and said, "Just remember, boys. Keep it in your pants."

[Brief aside: I paused for the laugh that I expected, but there was silence. I thought that the story had missed its mark, but just as I went to move on, a dull chuckle started to ease out in the packed church. The chuckle grew into an uproar of laughter. Even the priests were laughing.]

In closing, I just want to express to you that my family doesn't want you to mourn my mother's death but to celebrate her life and her laughter.

Joellen Vanvliet's Eulogy

Carmie came into my life about thirty years ago when she married my uncle. We have always been close, but it has been over the past eight years or so that she became more than just my aunt. She became a trusted friend and a confidant. Carmie always prayed to St. Therese, the little flower. If you've ever read about St. Therese, you know that she talked about "great love." Carmie's great love is her three boys. So, it was over countless glasses of chardonnay and endless, competitive games of Scrabble that I would tell

Carmie of my hope to receive the same love that she had from her boys, from my own two boys as they grew into young men. Carmie always assured me that I would. I gave Carmie a prayer card not too long ago, and I would like to share it with you all today. When you read it, please think of Carmie as the angel.

"May you always have an angel by your side, watching out for you, helping you believe in brighter days and in dreams come true, giving you comfort and courage—someone to catch you if you fall, inspiring smiles, holding your hand, and helping through it all. May you always have an angel—Carmie—by your side."

Good-bye, Carmie, I will miss you.

I will always remember and cherish the love and kindness that we received from our friends and relatives at the gravesite. Most of all, I will always remember my good friend, Father Moe. He said some prayers and again spoke about Carmie's toughness and about how much Carmie loved and cared for everyone. "Carmie is still laughing," he said. "I have never done this before, but I feel like doing it now. Hip, hip, hooray, everybody. Hip, hip, hooray!" We all chanted, "Hip, hip, hooray" three times. Carmie was making us laugh, even at her grave. I am sure that Carmie's laughter rang out through the heavens. The bagpipers stood off to the side and played "Amazing Grace." I had to fight back tears when I looked to the side and saw Matt, Pat, and Scott consoling one another. They were hugging, crying, and laughing at the same time. Again, I thought of Carmie's last words: "We did a good job."

# Chapter 24

# Laughing, Loving, Caring

The days following the funeral were the loneliest days of my life. As they passed, I began to feel Carmie's presence in my heart and soul. I remember her friend Pat telling me, "When you lie in bed at night, feel yourself holding her hand. Talk to her! She is still with you." I especially feel her laughing, loving, and caring through our wonderful sons for whom we had lived our entire lives. "We did a good job!"

Oftentimes, Carmie's wonderful friends invited our family to their homes for dinner or a cocktail. At first it was very difficult for us to be with Carmie's friends, because we missed her love and laughter. There was always that empty chair. As time passed, her friends brought us great joy and consolation and helped us to keep Carmie in our lives.

Carmie's friends had a bench built as a memorial to her life. On one side of the bench are the words "Carmie Brady, Forever a Junior." On the other side are three hearts and the words "Laughing, Loving, Caring." When the bench arrived at my house, I invited all of her friends to come to sit on it and share the peace and joy that I felt. Just as the burning bush was a sign of God's presence to the Israelites, the bench is a sign of Carmie's presence and love for all of us.

The bench now sits in a place of honor on the north end of the boardwalk at Point Pleasant Beach, New Jersey, for all to sit on and pray. To this day, I begin my day by walking on the boardwalk. When I finish walking, I sit on the bench and talk to Carmie. "Thank you, Carmie, for having blessed me and the boys with your love. You are such a wonderful mother and wife." Then I end each session with the prayer, "Come with me, Carmie. Walk with me through this day. Bless us in this life as you have always done in the past." Whenever someone asks me to pray for them, I sit on that bench and pray that God will bless them and watch over them. There are times when I have trodden through two feet of snow to get to the bench to feel her presence and to pray for those in need. I never feel her presence in the cemetery. I feel her loving presence here at the bench and throughout my day.

If ever you are feeling lonely, sad, desperate, or in need of consolation and love, sit on Carmie's bench and talk to Carmie and to God.

## Chapter 25

# Carmie's Prayer

Over the next couple of years, I came to realize how much Carmie's love for God, our Blessed Mother, and St. Therese meant to so many of her friends. Over and over I hear people say, "I am praying to Carmie to help me with my burdens. I am praying to Carmie to help me get a job. I am praying to Carmie for my sick mother or aunt or child." I began to understand that I was not doing enough to reach out and help those who needed to feel Carmie's laughing, loving, and caring. People needed to know that they could always reach Carmie and God through prayer.

One night I woke up from a deep sleep and found myself talking to Carmie in the form of a prayer: I immediately got out of bed and wrote down the words. Scott read the prayer and printed it on a card for all to pray. I don't care if people think I'm crazy. I give the prayer card to anyone who is in need of Carmie's love.

Carmie Brady
March 12, 1952–May 21, 2004
Laughing, Loving, Caring

Dear Carmie,

You were strong in the face of adversity because of your unyielding faith in God. Through that faith, you were the beneficiary of many miracles. At age twenty-eight, you overcame certain death at the birth of your first son and were blessed with two more. At age thirty-five, you were given two months to live when you were diagnosed with a rare form of breast cancer. Through your faith, determination, and God's will, you were cured and lived cancer-free for over fifteen years. At age forty-eight, you battled ovarian cancer for many years, because your mission in life was not completed. Your last words, to me, "We did a good job," sum up your life.

Dear Carmie, we now know that your life has not ended but has merely changed. We still hear your laughter, feel the warmth of your love, and know that you are still caring for us in our times of adversity, illness, fear, sadness, and hardship. Bestow upon us your courage to laugh in the face of adversity, to love in the face of sadness and loneliness, and to care about ourselves and about those who are most in need of God's love. We ask you to intercede for us with St. Therese and Jesus, that God may grant this special favor. Amen.

# CHAPTER 26

# Miracles

Carmie was the recipient of numerous miracles during her life. Now she has become the instrument through which God is bestowing miracles upon her family and friends. After Carmie died, I spoke to her secretary on the phone. I mentioned the balloons that were released into the sky the day after her death. I described how her friends had stood in awe as the balloons that had soared off into the horizon returned and hovered over them.

Carmie's secretary told me that she herself had often sat in wonderment at some of the things she witnessed when Carmie cared for her clients. "It was almost as if she was performing miracles during her lifetime. She even helped to cure a woman who suffered from multiple personalities." The secretary went on to tell me, "Keep track of everything that happens." The secretary was foretelling what I now know. God is using Carmie as His agent to bestow His miracles upon those Carmie left behind.

Here are some of the miraculous stories I have collected.

## A Path of Roses

On the first anniversary of Carmie's passing to her new life, Father Moe celebrated a Mass at our home for Carmie's close relatives and friends. For personal reasons,

Scott was not able to attend the Mass. Each of us grieves in his own way and must be free to seek out peace as his needs dictate.

"On the morning of the anniversary," Scott said, "I went up to the beach and said some prayers at Mom's favorite spot." Whenever Carmie was despondent or needed to be close to God, she sat on that same spot on the beach for hours and meditated and talked to God, our Blessed Mother, and St. Therese.

Scott continued, "Dad, I took three dozen roses to the beach because I knew how much Mom loves roses. I said some prayers and talked to Mom. I told her, 'These roses are for you, Mom. I love you.' I tossed the roses into the ocean as a gift of my love. I thought they would spread out as a beautiful collage in Mom's memory. Much to my disappointment, the roses remained in a clump and soon disappeared into the sea. I knew Mom was laughing, so I laughed along with her and said, 'I'm sorry, Mom. I'll do better next time.'

"I lay back on the beach and talked to Mom. I must have fallen asleep. After a long time, I woke up and talked to Mom again. Then I got up and walked aimlessly along the waterfront, deep in thought, alone and sad. As I strolled along the beach, I noticed something that had washed ashore. It was in the sand about fifty yards in front of me. As I approached the object, I was elated and overjoyed to see that one of Mom's roses had washed back to shore. It was as if Mom was talking and laughing. 'Hi, Scott, I am still with you! You are not alone!'

"I walked about a hundred yards further and spotted another beautiful rose. My tears turned to joy; my loneliness gave way to feeling Mom's presence and love. I could hear her laughter over the sound of the waves. I walked for at least a mile, and every two hundred or so yards there was a rose waiting for me. It was if Mom was making a path for me to follow."

I listened in awe to Scott's words and descriptions of the miracle that had taken place. I later got on my knees and thanked God and Carmie for creating a path that would lead Scott through the darkest periods in his life. Jesus said, "I am the way, the truth, and the light." Carmie was showing Scott that the path through life leads to eternal happiness.

## A Child Is Healed

I had a lunch date with Dr. Dwyer. When he did not show up, I called his office. "Didn't you hear?" said the nurse. "The doctor rushed down to Virginia. His grandson is dying." Frantically, I called his relatives to find out his daughter's phone number.

The daughter answered and put Dr. Dwyer on the phone. With the sound of terror in his voice, he uttered, "Charley, please pray for my eight-year-old grandson. He was must have been bitten by some kind of bug and is in a coma and convulsing violently. We think it might be brain encephalitis or meningitis. It doesn't look good. He is dying."

"Pat," I said, "did you pray to Carmie?"

In the background, I heard him say to his wife, "Patty, come here. Charley said to pray to Carmie. Why didn't we think of that?" He got back on the phone and said, "I'll call you later. We are going to pray to Carmie."

Later that night, he called me. "Charley, as soon as we got off the phone, Patty and I got on our knees and prayed to Carmie like we never prayed before."

Two years later—while attending a Mass celebrated at my house on the third anniversary of Carmie's passing—Dr. Dwyer and his wife shared the ending to their grandson's story. At the end of the Mass, he asked to speak. He told of Matthew's miraculous birth and about the breast cancer that was miraculously healed. He told about the number of times that Carmie mysteriously went into remission during her bout with ovarian cancer.

"Carmelinda Brady is the strongest person that I have ever known," he said. "Her faith is unparalleled. The fact that Carmie and Matthew are alive is truly a miracle." He then went on to relate the events that had taken place with his grandson in Virginia. "The boy was in a coma and dying. There was no hope. We were desperate. In the midst of our desperation, we received a phone call from Charley, who immediately asked, 'Did you pray to Carmie?' Patty and I immediately got down on our knees and prayed to Carmie.

"Later that day, we returned to the hospital, and it was just like in the movies. The child was out of the coma and the convulsions had stopped—at the exact time that we had prayed to Carmie."

A twenty-two-year-old young man told me about a miracle that was bestowed upon him as a result of his prayers to Carmie. Here are his words.

## Roses Mend the Heart

In early September of 2006, I was told that I needed open-heart surgery. At first it was not a big deal to me. I looked upon it as a simple surgery and felt that I would be fine. After a week or two, with my mom doing tons of research, we learned that there were only two surgeons in the country who could perform this delicate and rare operation.

As I approached the date of my surgery, it started to take a toll on me mentally. I was stressing out, losing weight, and had extreme anxiety attacks. The Monday before I actually left to go to the hospital, my mom told me that there was a "healing" Mass that day and suggested I go. All day I debated whether or not I should go, because honestly I thought it was a waste of time. When I returned home and got out of my car that day, I finally decided I would not go.

Now, this is where I sensed the first "presence" of Carmie. As soon as I opened the door of the house, I was bombarded by the strongest scent of roses. At first I just thought that a candle was burning or that potpourri was sitting out. But the smell followed me all the way into the kitchen to where my father was. I asked him if he smelled the roses, and he didn't. He actually stood right beside me and could not smell the scent.

At that point, I thought of it as a sign from Carmie and I went to the healing Mass. More than anything, the Mass served as the peace of mind that helped me cope and accept what was going to happen.

The next morning, I was on my way to work when my mom contacted me and asked me if I wanted to go with Chuck Brady to Carmie's healer, Maria. Without hesitation, I said yes. Chuck picked me up and drove me to the healer. On the way to the house, he told me the story and background of Carmie's life from when she was first diagnosed with cancer. The whole time, even to this day, I remember having the chills throughout my body.

When we got to the healer's house, I lay down on the bed, and she began the session. This is where I believe Carmie again showed her presence. I don't believe I ever fell asleep, because I was conscious of my surroundings. But during the session, I had a dream of Carmie and her son Pat. The three of us were on the beach. Actually, I think it was a memory of our trip to St. Thomas, but the dream came out of nowhere. At that specific time, my session actually kind of scared me. My body started to twitch uncontrollably, and I had a sensation of warmth and felt as if I was floating. The following day, I received a newspaper article from Chuck about Carmie and a picture of the rose that bloomed on the day Matt was born.

Later, I was in Rochester, and it was the morning of my surgery. I prepped as instructed and showered. Again, I felt the strong presence of Carmie. As soon as I dried off and opened the bathroom door, I was overwhelmed by the beautiful odor of roses—which, again, my father couldn't smell. That day we waited for hours, but the surgery was canceled and rescheduled for the following Tuesday.

That Tuesday morning I couldn't sleep. I was very restless. I remember lying in the bed just staring up at the ceiling. Out of nowhere, my dad in the next bed started screaming and saying, "Who is that? What are you saying?"

I asked him, "Who are you talking to? Is it Carmie?" But he wouldn't answer me. When it was time for me to start prepping again, I jumped into the shower.

This is when the last presence of Carmie came to me. I followed the same routine as the previous time. I got out of the shower, dried off, and opened the door. Again, I was overwhelmed by the smell of roses. This time my father was not there, but my mother was. I told her about the smell. She walked toward me, and she too smelled the very strong scent of roses. That time, it was a most relaxing and heartwarming presence. It put both my mother and me at ease. At that point, I truly knew it was Carmie, and I was no longer nervous. I knew that I was going to be okay. The operation was a complete success. I have returned to a normal life and thank Carmie and God every day.

I recently met up with that young man. He proudly showed me the red roses that he had tattooed on his shoulder in remembrance of Carmie.

The next account is from a young mother.

## Congenital Heart Defect

On January 28, 2010, 6:18 a.m., our world changed forever. Our newborn son let out the most beautiful cry, and I was beaming because, at that moment, I had become the mother of my second son. Every moment after the first brought a much different feeling.

Doctors determined that our son was born with a congenital heart defect called "transposition of the great arteries." He needed to be transported immediately to another hospital where he was to undergo open-heart surgery. His heart—and that of our family's—was broken. How could this have happened? What were we going to do? I knew only one "person" had those answers. I was going to have to have faith.

Aiden's stay was twenty-eight days long. It was agonizing to see my child in pain with no way for me to fix it. Throughout this ordeal, my husband and I prayed, and we prayed hard and long. We prayed for answers and strength—and for healing, mostly. I prayed at my baby's bedside daily to God, to saints, and to those I felt closely connected to—guardian angels. One of the strongest, kindest and most mothering of those angels was Carmie Brady, or Mrs. Brady, to me. I knew that if anyone would understand and had any clout "up above," it would be Mrs. Brady. Every time I felt a sense of peace and calm, I knew she was there.

Things improved throughout the year with minor setbacks, and again we leaned on prayer. We had adjusted to life at the doctor's office to make sure Aiden's heart would continue to be strong. No one knows how, with each visit, my stomach ached, my heart pounded, and my mind raced awaiting bad news.

Then in early January, I received a post on my Facebook account from Charles Brady. He wrote, "I am going to Carmie's bench today, and I will pray for your beautiful son Aiden." Gratitude ran through me, and so did a calm feeling.

Aiden's final appointment with the cardiologist was January 19, 2011. It was the first time he was given clearance for six whole months before he had to go back. Call it what you will. Aiden has many angels guiding him through the good and the bad. I am lucky to know one of those amazing angels: Carmie Brady. I know those angels healed my son, and I am forever thankful.

# CHAPTER 27

# Walk for the Cure

In order to understand how the Carmie Brady Foundation came about, we must first flash back to an event that took place about fifteen years prior to Carmie's death. Carmie was still suffering from the ravages of the breast cancer operation and the treatments. One beautiful Sunday afternoon, Carmie and her friend Eileen burst into the house. They proceeded to open a bottle of wine, laughing boisterously.

When I inquired as to what the celebration was about, Carmie joyfully responded. "Chuck," she said, "we just participated in the Walk for the Cure, which is sponsored by the American Cancer Society. We joined thousands of women, many of whom were suffering from cancer and many of whom had survived it. It was a beautiful day and a beautiful event."

I immediately felt terrible. "Why didn't you tell me and the boys?" I asked. "We would have walked with you."

"Next year," Carmie said, "we'll all walk together."

The following year, Carmie and Eileen again "walked for the cure." This time, the boys and I and about thirty of Carmie's friends and relatives donned "Brady Bunch" shirts and walked with them. Carmie's good friend Beth made a Brady Bunch sign and led us through the walk. About three quarters of the way through the walk, we were surrounded by beautiful butterflies that followed us to the end. Tradition has it that butterflies are a sign of God's presence. Little did we know that a tradition was born for the Brady Bunch that would continue on into the future.

After the walk, we returned to the Brady home for a victory party. Carmie continued to participate in the walk up until the year she died. I will always remember her last walk. Despite the fact that she was so weak that she could hardly speak or walk, she laughed and greeted the nearly two hundred friends who came out to join her. Her beautiful laughter and her loving spirit pierced through the howling wind and the bitter cold and brought joy and laughter to all of her friends.

Once again, we were joined by our beautiful friends, the butterflies, who seemed to be telling us: "God is with you and loves you. Do not fret. Rejoice and be happy." Again, Carmie invited everyone back to the house for the traditional victory party. Two hundred loved ones shared in her customary laughing, loving, and caring.

The tradition continues to this day. Carmie passed into eternal life on May 21, 2004, but the influence of her life on this earth goes on. By the third year after her passing, the throng had grown to over three hundred people. Many of them had never met or known Carmie. By then, we had become more organized. We had our own signup table and collected donations for the cure. Proudly wearing our Brady Bunch shirts, we tacked onto the end of the main contingent. When we arrived at the boardwalk, we paused at Carmie's bench.

The boys handed out a red rose to each participant—just like the red rose that bloomed on the day of the miraculous birth of Carmie's first son—and Matt said a prayer.

Then the Pipes and Drums of the Jersey Shore led us down the boardwalk. When we arrived at our destination, the pipers separated into two columns and proceeded to play "Amazing Grace." Last year, almost five hundred people joyfully walked between the pipers, holding their roses high above their heads as a sign of victory over death and this dreaded disease. The tears flowing from our eyes accompanied endless smiles because we knew in our hearts that Carmie was still with us. Through her friends and loved ones, she was still laughing, loving, and caring.

**Pipes and Drums of the Jersey Shore.**

# CHAPTER 28

# Hope Lodge

Thrilled by the fact that we had raised $9,000, we invited a member of the American Cancer Society to meet with us to determine how the money would be spent. The boys were emphatic. "We do not want this money to be used for salaries. Our mother would want it to be used for something special." We were invited to tour Hope Lodge, which is a beautiful new building in New York, sponsored by the American Cancer Society. Executives at the ACS proudly showed us around the building and explained to us that anyone who was undergoing treatment for cancer at any hospital in New York could stay free of charge with their loved ones.

The boys immediately thought of the many times they had seen me drive their mother back and forth to New York for treatments. I overheard one of the boys ask, "Can we sponsor a room at Hope Lodge in our mother's name? This is where we want the $9,000 to go."

The gentleman was kind in his response. "We do have sponsorships, but you would have to pledge $100,000, paid at $20,000 a year over a five-year period."

I immediately interjected, "I overheard your conversation. I will take the additional $11,000 out of my pension this year, and we will raise the $20,000 at the walk each year." Deeply touched by the offer of these young men, he turned to the other executives and emotionally informed them that the Brady Bunch had pledged $100,000 to sponsor the Carmie Brady Room at Hope Lodge.

123

**Matt, Chuck, Scott at Carmie Brady Room in Hope Lodge**

The following year, we raised $17,500 and made the $20,000 payment. In 2009, we woke up to howling winds and torrential rain. The weather was so bad that only 150 people braved the weather and walked for the cure. How would we come up with the $20,000 pledge?

We rented a tent for the victory party. To our joy, over two hundred additional people showed up at the house. People who could not attend sent donations via our Web site and through the mail. We are happy to report that, in 2009, we mailed our third $20,000 donation to Hope Lodge. In 2011, we were joined by almost five hundred friends and made our fifth $20,000 contribution to Hope Lodge.

There is no end to this book. Carmie will walk with us forever. "O death, where is thy sting?" The patients at Hope Lodge will share in her life of laughing, loving, and caring forever.

I would like to share an experience that I had while visiting Hope Lodge. The manager knocked on the door of the Carmie Brady Room and introduced me as Carmie Brady's husband and a member of the "Brady Bunch." The gentleman inside the room immediately hugged me and invited me into his temporary home. He showed me around the room as if it were his castle. With tears in his eyes, he uttered, "I would like to introduce you to my wife, but she just returned from treatments and is too ill to talk." The poor woman was apparently writhing in pain. He continued, "I cannot thank you enough for what you have done for me and my wife. Prior to learning about Hope Lodge, we had given up all hope. We could no longer afford to come to New York for treatments. Thanks to you and the Brady Bunch, our hope has been restored." Again, he hugged me and cried. "Go back and tell the Brady Bunch how much I love them."

# Chapter 29

# Birth of the
# Carmie Brady Foundation

It was October of 2006. Carmie had passed away in 2004. We had just completed our fifteenth Walk for the Cure. The victory party had subsided, and a few friends were sitting around in my yard reminiscing about Carmie's life. We began to talk about the wonderful success that we'd had with the walk and about the good that we were accomplishing in Carmie's name. One of my sons exclaimed, "If we could raise all of this money in one day, think of the good that we could do in Mom's name if we had a charitable foundation." Another son joyfully proclaimed, "Mom's life of laughing, loving, and caring would live on forever." We were encouraged by our good friends Rob Clayton, Sandy Leibfried, and Dan Decorcia, who agreed to be on the founding board of trustees.

After many months of meetings, discussions, and prayer, the Carmie Brady Foundation was born. We applied for and received our 501(c) 3 designation and were on our way. After that, we needed a goal.

"Mom loved little children," Pat remarked. "She would want to help sick children." We decided to run two fundraisers a year. The first would be the Walk for the Cure, which would raise money for the Carmie Brady Room at Hope Lodge. The second would be a gala fundraiser. Pat suggested, "Every cent that we raise will be donated to families who are struggling to survive financially because of the fact that they have a seriously ill child."

The first annual fundraiser was held on the third week of June in 2008. Over 350 joyful people took part in what turned out to be a beautiful celebration and continuance of the life of Carmie Brady. Carmie's spirit permeated the air in which we celebrated. Over and over again, friends would come up to us and exclaim, "Carmie is with us today. I can feel her love and concern for sick children. I can hear her laughter."

The fourth annual fundraiser , which was held in April of 2011, was attended by over four hundred and fifty people. All of the money that was raised is being distributed to families who are struggling to make ends meet because of the expenses of raising a seriously ill child.

## The End Is Just the Beginning

There is no end to Carmie Brady's legacy of laughing, loving, and caring. Carmie lives on—in and through the wonderful volunteers who make up the Carmie Brady Foundation. As long as there are sick people in the world, the foundation will continue to reach out to them. Carmie's love will reach into Hope Lodge and into the homes of seriously ill children. We will always hear her laughter in the Walk for the Cure and the annual fundraiser. Families of seriously ill children and patients in Hope Lodge will feel the warmth of her love and know how much she and the Lord care for them through the good deeds of the Carmie Brady Foundation and our sponsors and volunteers.

To date, the Carmie Brady Foundation has raised over $100,000 for Hope Lodge and $150,000 that has helped numerous families who are struggling to keep their heads above water as a result of caring for a seriously ill child.

All of this work is being accomplished by a small group of volunteers who donate their time and money out of the goodness of their hearts. There are no salaries. There is no compensation—except for the knowledge that we are helping our fellow human beings.

If you would like to learn more about the Carmie Brady Foundation or make a donation, please go to www.carmiebradyfoundation.com or contact us at the Carmie Brady Foundation, P.O. Box 91, Manasquan, NJ 08736.

## Note from the Author

It is my sincere hope that all who read this book will receive some hope and inspiration from the life and example of Carmie Brady. In your time of need, may her laughter cheer you up, and may her love bring you closer to God. May you forever feel her caring nature.

I am having this book published so that people all over the world will be inspired by Carmie's life. It is my pledge to you that one hundred percent of the profits that are derived from this book will be donated to the Carmie Brady Foundation, which will continue to sponsor the Carmie Brady Room at Hope Lodge and to help the parents of seriously ill children.

If you would like to share your thoughts or suggestions with me personally, please contact me at charles.brady1@yahoo.com. I would love to hear from you. You can be sure that I will always keep you in my prayers. May God always be with you and bless you.

Sincerely,

Charles A Brady
Husband   Author

Made in the USA
San Bernardino, CA
25 August 2014